"Marsha Geoghagan's book, *Destined for Destruction, but Love Stepped In*, may save your life! Darkness is real, but the name and blood of Jesus are stronger. Reading this book will equip you to do anything Marsha can do."

SID ROTH
Host, *It's Supernatural!*

"Marsha Geoghagan's story *Destined for Destruction, but Love Stepped In* unfolds like a captivating television series. Her stories are a testimony to what faith and courage will bring anyone through. Marsha will show you the goodness of God and His faithfulness through challenges most of us haven't had to face as He rescues her time and time again. A fast read -- to find out what happens next."

LONNIE LANE
Host, *Waiting For Messiah*
www.Lonnielane.blogspot.com

"With a life slogan of "trust Jesus," Marsha journeys through heartbreak, darkness, pain, and supernatural encounters, all the while experiencing the powerful workings of the Holy Spirit at a deeper and deeper level. *Destined for Destruction, but Love Stepped In* will encourage and inspire anyone who has ever questioned God's purpose for their life, walked through abusive relationships, struggled as a parent, or ever felt like giving up. Marsha's story is one of hope, perseverance, faith, and an ever-increasing passion to know God in the most personal, intimate way possible."

BRAD CREWS
Pastor
Celebration Church of Orange Park

"I have known Marsha for twenty-three years. It is an honor to write an endorsement for this book. I first was introduced to this unusually anointed lady at TBN in Jacksonville, Florida in December 1994. I was scheduled to be a guest on the program. On arrival, I was introduced to Marsha, and I knew immediately we were kindred spirits. Before the program started, she gathered the guests together to pray. This woman of God prayed down the fire. The Holy Spirit was all over us as we asked God to move in power in our city.

"I moved to Jacksonville a year later and thus begun a friendship which has grown and flourished over these years. Marsha is preacher who hasn't forgotten her meagre beginnings. She overflows with the love of Christ for everyone she comes across. Her story inside these covers is a story of how our amazing God makes beauty from ashes. She is a trophy of the amazing grace of the amazing God that she serves. Marsha walks out the Scriptures on a daily basis.

"I totally believe that God will use this book for His Glory. Many souls will come to Christ through this book. Many will receive deliverance, and many will receive the baptism in the Holy Spirit and fire. I conclude with the Scripture she hangs onto many times from Romans 8v28: *And we know that in all things God works for the good of those who love him, who have been called according to his purpose.*"

DR. D. ALLAN WIGGINS
Set Free by the Sea Ministries

DESTINED FOR DESTRUCTION, BUT LOVE STEPPED IN

MARSHA GEOGHAGAN

Storehouse Media Group, LLC
Jacksonville, FL

DESTINED FOR DESTRUCTION, BUT LOVE STEPPED IN

Copyright © 2018 by Marsha Geoghagan

All rights reserved. No part of this publication may be reproduced, distributed, or transmitted in any form or by any means, including photocopying, recording, or other electronic or mechanical methods, without the prior written permission of the publisher, except in the case of brief quotations embodied in critical reviews and certain other noncommercial uses permitted by copyright law. For permission requests, write to the publisher, addressed "Attention: Permissions Coordinator," at the email address below.

Storehouse Media Group, LLC
Jacksonville, Florida
www.StorehouseMediaGroup.com
Author@StorehousePublishers.com

Ordering Information:

Quantity sales: Special discounts are available on quantity purchases by corporations, associations, and others. For details, contact the "Special Sales Department" at the email address above.

The views expressed in this work are solely those of the author and do not necessarily reflect the views of the publisher, and the publisher hereby disclaims any responsibility for them.

Destined for Destruction but Love Stepped In / Marsha Geoghagan. —1st ed.

ISBN: 978-1-943106-30-1 (paperback)
ISBN: 978-1-943106-35-6 (hardcover)
ISBN: 978-1-943106-31-8 (ebook)

Library of Congress Control Number: 2018943067

Printed in the United States of America

DEDICATION

I pondered on how to start this dedication page. I wondered what the difference between thanking and dedicating. Dedicating is a committed to task or purpose.

First, I dedicate this book to the Holy Spirit. Without His Life within me, there would be no book. Really, there would be no Marsha.

Second, I dedicate this book to Lee Geoghagan, my longtime friend, who is my husband. God has saved the best for the last. He is my safe place to land. He lets me be me and has accepted the fact that he married a "crowd" and loves all of us in spite of the chaos. There are not enough words to say what my heart feels for you.

Last but not least, I dedicate this book to my five children, DeAnna, Ricky, Scotty, Erika, and Jazz. You are and always will be my life. The Bible said, "Life is in the blood." How true that is.

EPIGRAPH

"And we know that God causes everything to work together for good of those who love God and are called according to His purpose for them."

>   --Romans 8:28 (New Living Translation)

Faith Under Pressure:

2-4 Consider it a sheer gift, friends, when tests and challenges come at you from all sides. You know that under pressure, your faith-life is forced into the open and shows its true colors. So, don't try to get out of anything prematurely. Let it do its work so you become mature and well-developed, not deficient in any way.

>   **--James 1:2 The Message Bible**

Table of Contents

Chapter One: INTRIGUING PROPOSALS 1
Chapter Two: STOPPING FOR A HAMBURGER 12
Chapter Three: THE BAND 17
Chapter Four: THE TRIP 24
Chapter Five: THE BITES 35
Chapter Six: THE RETURN 41
Chapter Seven: DO YOU KNOW JESUS? 45
Chapter Eight: I FOUND HIM 54
Chapter Nine: THE PROPHECY 64
Chapter Ten: AN ANGEL AND STITCHES 77
Chapter Eleven: GRANDMA'S HOUSE 93
Chapter Twelve: REGRETFUL TO REJOICING 107
Chapter Thirteen: THE DREAM 124
Chapter Fourteen: MARSHA'S GHOST 134
Chapter Fifteen: EVERY DOG HAS ITS DAY 147
Chapter Sixteen: CHALLENGES AND MORE 157
Chapter Seventeen: "YOU NEED TO DIVORCE ME" 170
Chapter Eighteen: MURDER AND THE BLOOD 178
Chapter Nineteen: TELEVISION 196
Chapter Twenty: FAITHFUL IS MY GOD 211

About the Author: MARSHA GEOGHAGAN 219

Foreword

DESTINED FOR DESTRUCTION BUT LOVE STEPPED IN is truly a book you will not want to put down. In a unique style, Marsha leads the reader on a journey which can be described as fascinating, riveting, captivating, entertaining, stimulating, thought-provoking, and intriguing. Her style of writing will definitely keep your attention as you join her on a journey, which will have your jaw dropping.

I remember sitting in a pizza restaurant many years ago in Jacksonville, Florida. Across from me was my friend Marsha, who began to share a lot of what you will be reading in this book. I was listening and was amazed at what she was telling me. I thought, *Is she for real? Can this all be true? This is unbelievable!*

Many years later I can assure you that the answers to the above questions are yes. We are all on a journey with the same destination. **DESTINED FOR DESTRUCTION BUT LOVE STEPPED IN** is the love story of the ages. Jesus has revealed His love, character, and nature over and over through this adventurous love story.

You will love the book, and if you ever have the privilege of meeting Marsha and getting to know her, you will know you have just spent time with love who stepped in.

It has been a privilege and honor to know her and watch the Master's hand on her life's journey.

–Nancy Kaplan
Founder, Gates of Prayer Ministries
Author, *Turn the Battle at the Gate*

Acknowledgments

I have read Acknowledgment pages in several books. Sometimes, I just skipped over them, thinking, *Oh, it's nice to mention their names.* But after writing my book, I am ashamed that I assumed it was just a nice jester. Oh, how important those people were to the author.

I'll start with my five children, who endured this journey with me. Thank you to DeAnna Adamson and her husband Mike, Ricky Yarbrough and his wife Denise, Scott Yarbrough, Erika Yarbrough, and Jazz Yarbrough. My love for each of you can never be measured, and how proud I am of each. Our family has an amazing gift of loving in the hardest times and forgiving when the wrong seems unforgivable. You are just like Jesus. I am proud that God allowed me to birth each of you.

I want to thank my grandchildren for listening to their grandma talk about Jesus over and over again: Garrett and Danielle Adamson Deven and Ruby Yarbrough, Sierra and Caleb Gibson, Dane Yarbrough, Haili Yarbrough, Fallyn Yarbrough, Seth Wysocki, Aidan Yarbrough, and Waylon Jolly. The DNA of our family runs deep in each of you with unique traits that many other families wish they had.

Thank you to my great-grands Isai, Layla, Ezra, Levi. Because of you, this family's future still goes forth.

Thank you to my husband's daughters LaDonna and her husband Ronny Mensforth, Jennifer and her husband Derrick Porter and their children Emma and Alana Mensforth, and Sienna and Dylan Porter for accepting me with love.

Thank you to two special sisters, Carol Mattingly and Debbie Kidwell, whose generous spirits and laughter believed in me. Thank you, Margie Ussery and Charlene Davis, for reading my manuscript in its raw and unedited state and encouraging me with your words, "I couldn't stop reading it." Your feedback kept me writing.

Thank you to my Aglow ladies Joyce Hlad, Carol Ansley, Pat Thomas, and Debbie Vinciguerra for your friendship, prayers, and laughter that I so needed.

Thank you to all of my Orange Park Celebration Church friends for your smiles and for loving me, regardless of what had and would come out of my mouth. So polite you were. And thank you for the love each of you demonstrated during a time when His love was needed in my family's life at the celebration of the memorial for my son Scott. This gratitude includes Mary Horner, Tonya Shelton, John Rogers, Orlando Anido, and so many more.

Thank you to Pastor Mark and Faith Souter of Set Free by the Sea Ministries. Your love for the least of them showed Scott who Jesus truly was. Mercy stepped in and took him home. Forever grateful.

Thank you to my family at WJEB—Colette Snowden, Carolyn Rentrope, Clayton Roney, Rondy Watson, and Darius Brown. We are certainly family. I can never say how much your love and understanding, along with the comfort you gave me when Scott went to heaven, have meant to me.

Thank you to my editors for all the hard work you've done on my book. Thanks to Sherrie Clark for performing a developmental edit in the beginning and then subsequent edits. I will be forever indebted to your expertise and friendship. And thank you to Lonnie Lane and Nancy Kaplan for the edits you did. I also want to thank

Storehouse Media Group for taking my book through the publishing process to the finished product it is today.

Thank you to my lovely cousin Lyn Brosowski, who posted morning pictures of the city I love—Jerusalem—from her balcony to start my day, reminding me that Jesus (Yeshua) will return soon.

Thank you to Angi and Donnie Greenway, Lionel Staplefoote, Ruth Bannon, Patty Powell, Jennifer Cummings, Barbara Adamson, Bonnie Mays, Angel Brown, Cherry Fulford, Judy Roumillat, and Brenda Mackey, to just name a few, for being a blessing in my life from long ago to now. If I have left anyone out, it was not on purpose. Each of you means so much to me.

Thank you to Stacy Ramos who knows all too well the unseen realm. We share a common bond with this. We have laughed and shook our heads at the unbelievable, unexplainable Holy Spirit as we just kept asking if this could be true. What an adventure.

Thank you to the ONE WHO spoke to me many years ago to write His Story through my vessel, not for me but for the world to understand that His love always brings you to the destination that is for your good.

Thank you to all of you who I have the honor to call friends. I hope that anyone who reads this book will be able to say, "Now I know that all things will work out for my good because I can trust in that unseen person."

Shalom,
Marsha

Chapter One

INTRIGUING PROPOSALS

My head spun while driving my yellow 1967 Ford Fairlane north on Interstate 95.

I couldn't stop thinking about the previous night's conversation with my ex-husband, who now lived in California. He had asked me to move out there with the kids. I don't know why his words wouldn't leave my mind. After all, I had already paid a heavy price with him, so why even consider this?

Although we had been divorced for two years, I couldn't forget how our relationship broke me in many ways. In the beginning, it cost me my innocence, and subsequently, it introduced me to an unknown life. Throughout it all, I felt I had been shortchanged.

My thoughts turned to the summer of 1963, when we first met. I once read that certain memories involved more details and therefore took up more space, and my brain was overflowing because memories of him definitely involved more details.

Details! What a way to start a Monday.

Oh well. I decided to try to concentrate on getting to work and letting the week begin. I drove past the airport terminal, trying to evade the road construction. As I passed the billboard that read "New and Improved International Airport," I wondered when this new and improved airport would finally be completed.

I did have to acknowledge that the City of Jacksonville, Florida was changing.

"Change is good," I said. "Yep, change is good."

I took the side road past the main airport terminal, which led to a large cement-block building divided into different-sized warehouses or storage spaces. In front was a long loading dock running the length of the warehouses that faced a wooded area surrounding the airport.

I could see the names of different companies above their doors. The name that stood out the most was "Air Freight." Its sign stood over a corridor where trucks drove to the back of the building. Planes carrying freight unloaded directly to Air Freight at that location.

As I drove through the large parking lot, I waved at several of the guys. They stopped loading their trucks long enough to wave back.

I was one of three women who worked at these warehouses. My office was further down the building.

I pulled into my usual parking space, jogged up the stairs to the loading dock, and walked about eight feet to unlock my yellow metal office door. The only window to the outside world was the eight-by-fourteen-inch glass pane situated about eye level on that door.

The dimensions of my small office were comparable to a small storage unit rented by the month. It even had similar-looking concrete walls.

The room was only large enough to accommodate two desks with a chair in between. Mine was the first one, and a person had to walk past it to get to the second desk.

Mr. Hadley's son started this business. Although Mr. Hadley had another business, he helped his son run this one. I was their only employee. They delivered luggage to the homes or hotels of those passengers who lost them or left them behind at the airport. The father conducted most of the deliveries.

I had a good working relationship with both of them and enjoyed the job. I counted my solitude as a one-girl office to be a bonus. I especially welcomed being alone on this day. Thank goodness, I knew my job so well that I could perform it without thinking.

I walked into my office and switched on the lights. After setting my purse under the desk, I took a pen out of the pencil holder, clicked on the answer machine, and wrote the messages down on the message pad.

Thoughts of last night's conversation continued to haunt me. I had to be very careful because my thoughts bounced back and forth between positive and negative. Since I have always had an adventurous and impulsive spirit, my ability to think things through was greatly impaired. The urge to pack up and move to California was strong.

Looking back, I can see how at the age of twenty-four, I lacked maturity and wisdom when it came to relationships. The only mature and natural decisions I made at that time involved the raising of my children. Motherhood was natural to me, and I enjoyed it.

My lifelong dream consisted of getting married, raising children, and having a dog. Big goals, right? Well, to me they were. Admittedly, I married my ex-husband for all the wrong reasons, for the reasons an immature seventeen-year-old might choose. First, I started dating him because he was a good dancer. Not exactly a qualification for a husband, but at that time, it was an important quality for a boyfriend.

Due to peer pressure, I lost my virginity to him. After only having sex three times, I got pregnant the summer before my senior year of high school. I felt getting married was the right and moral thing to do. Both of us were too young, though, and the marriage turned out to be a disaster. In an effort to stabilize the marriage, we ended up having two more children. The problem was that I had tried to put a bandage on a wound that was bleeding out of control. It just didn't work out.

My thoughts were interrupted by a familiar voice coming through the door. "Good morning, Marsha."

I turned and smiled. "Good morning, Mr. Hadley."

He sat down in the hard-back chair, glanced at his watch, and adjusted his glasses. We engaged in small talk about the weather or some other trivial topic.

He then stood back up. I knew that meant he was leaving to start his deliveries. I handed him the list of addresses that I had already put in order.

I said, "We have five deliveries from last night's flights."

He smiled and walked toward the door.

I told him to have a good day as I watched him close the door behind him. I was somewhat relieved to be alone, except that I was left with the big question: should I or should I not go to California and start all over again?

I tried to focus on something besides my ex-husband's words: "You and the kids come to California. We can build a new life together."

Those words echoed louder than usual this day. Why couldn't I move past them? This was not the first time we'd had this conversation. The temptation was not about being with him. Instead, it was about making the drive across country to start fresh. The thought about taking three small kids on a cross-country road trip had never occurred to me until he called and made that suggestion.

Today, however, it was beginning to look like a possibility. I didn't want to renew my relationship with my ex-husband, but the journey to California sparked my adventurous spirit.

I picked through the invoices, trying to focus on the day ahead and making it to my lunchtime. The thought of my lunch hour stirred my emotions, and not because I was hungry. I felt somewhat excited about driving to the main airport terminal and using the payphone to call my ex-husband, because he was my only contact to California. I knew he would want to discuss last night's conversation again.

I could call from the office phone, but I didn't want to make a long-distance call from the office. Now that I had put a plan in place, my thoughts settled down.

The Stranger from the Supernatural Realm

As my fingers flew over the keys of the typewriter, I fell into the rhythm of their clicking sound. My mind kept to the beat with thoughts of expectancy and hope.

Suddenly, the door opened. A man with white hair and a light blue leisure suit walked through it.

I jerked my head up in surprise. "Can I help you?"

"I'm looking for Air Freight," he replied.

Puzzled, I said, "Air Freight is directly behind us, right down the corridor."

How could he miss Air Freight? They have the largest sign, and our office didn't have anything that would even indicate it was a business. Actually, from the outside, we looked like a vacant office.

He asked, "Do you mind if I use your phone to call California? I'm looking for some cargo to come in. I'll call collect."

I thought his request was unusual. Regardless, I pointed toward the phone on the other desk. "Go ahead."

I made myself look busy. I picked up the newly typed invoices, trying not to appear uneasy, and started to sort them.

After making his call, the stranger thanked me as he headed for the door. Then he stopped, placing both of his hands on my desk and leaning forward, closing the gap between us.

Fear jumped on me for the first time. The idea of rape hit me like a hammer. My body automatically recoiled backwards in my chair, only to be stopped by the cement wall behind me.

He said, "I have been sent to you."

Fear still gripped me, but those words seemed to ease my tension, if only a little. I was at his mercy with no way out. We were head to head now.

For the first time, I noticed the details of his face. I won't forget those eyes. They were the bluest of blue eyes, and they spoke without words. His thick, white hair contradicted his youthful face.

"I have been sent to you," he said again.

My mind usually moves at a fast pace, but it was as if my thoughts floated without an anchor. I wanted to respond and regain control, but many emotions surged within me. I found I couldn't question him.

He was very sure of himself, displaying an eerie self-confidence as he explained this abnormal visit. Again, I was spellbound, unable to ask questions.

"Right now," he said, "I am in California rehearsing with a choir, but I have astral projected to you."

He stepped back, placing his hands on top of his head. "Never let an entity come out of the top of your head," he explained. He then placed his hands on his chest. "You always come out from here. If you come out from the top of your head, another entity can come in."

I watched him, mesmerized by the atmosphere that engulfed him. He continued, speaking factually to me. "You are trying to make a decision." His steady blue eyes displayed his seriousness. He knew something that I had not spoken.

My mind went completely blank at his statement. I was unable to put up a defense to this stranger. He had invaded my brain without permission.

I struggled to open my mouth to defend my privacy, but he continued. "You were born in biblical days. You were very poor and had lots of children. You were in love with a Roman soldier."

Everything seemed to stand still. I wasn't certain if the air in the office had depleted. I couldn't relate to anything but this stranger who stood in front of me. This experience was way out of my league.

Who was this person? Why was he sent to me?

He continued to talk, but I couldn't comprehend anymore.

With utter self-assurance, he said, "You can also astral project to wherever or whenever you want."

I had never heard of astral projection at that time.

He said, "Walk with me outside to the loading dock."

I thought I would be safe if I complied and followed him. I had stopped feeling fearful and was now curious about this stranger's suggestions. My body automatically responded to his request. Without any more prompting, we left my office together.

The next thing I knew, we were standing beside each other on the loading dock. He was several inches taller than me. His blue eyes dazzled in the daylight like those of a doll.

"Do you see the aura that brings life to the trees?" He then pointed toward the woods. "Look with your spiritual eyes, not your physical ones. Everything in the universe has life to it. You will be able to understand this soon."

I didn't see anything, nor did I understand the terminology used by this stranger, but I was intrigued by this experience. He had captivated my adventurous spirit, and I took all of it in. Deep inside, I felt the inquisitive Marsha pulling on the logical Marsha. My defense barriers had tumbled down. I had now entered new territory.

Those first words he spoke to me, "I have been sent to you," were etched in my soul and reverberated in my mind. I wanted to ask, "Who sent you to me? And why?" But he held such a very strong presence that I couldn't muster up the courage to question him.

Everything about him caught me off guard. I was a young mother who had come from a normal family. I had a good upbringing with both parents. They had instilled good morals and taught us to always do the right things and treat people with respect. My parents lived the principles they taught.

I wasn't brought up in religion, but as a young child, I knew there was a God. I knew Jesus was His son. I went to church but was never forced to go. Up until then, the only real drama I had experienced in my young life was getting pregnant outside of marriage.

I tried squinting my eyes see with my "spiritual eyes." I wanted to see this aura that brought life to everything.

Mr. Hadley drove up. He stopped his car in front of the loading dock and stepped out. He leaned his forearm on top of the driver's door and asked me to recheck an address on an invoice.

When I turned to head back to the office, I heard the stranger greet Mr. Hadley like men do. I checked the invoice and walked back outside to convey the address to Mr. Hadley. He was still leaning casually on the car's door.

"Mr. Hadley," I said, not quite back to reality, "where did the man in the blue leisure suit go?"

"What man, Marsha?"

I laughed. "The man you were just talking with. You know, the white-haired man."

He climbed back into his car, saying with a smile and a giggle, "Hope you're not drinking this early."

I watched him leave the parking lot, all the while trying to grasp his response.

I immediately turned toward the corridor. My heels clicked on the pavement as I headed toward Air Freight.

Perhaps he was at Air Freight looking for his cargo. Surely, Mr. Hadley was just joking with me. He did have a sense of humor.

I entered the large open door and headed toward the receiving table to the warehouse's lead man. "Tom," I said, "I'm looking for the white-haired man in the blue leisure suit who's expecting cargo from California."

"Marsha, no one's been in here today," he said.

I couldn't hide my confusion and disbelief, and I knew my face gave these emotions away.

Several of the warehouse guys teased, "Marsha, we're the only man you need."

I thanked them, joking back, "You haven't seen this man?"

"No," Tom replied.

I walked back to my office feeling unbalanced, not so much physically but mentally. I opened the office door and walked in, not sure what I would find. Everything was exactly like before. There was no electricity shooting through the cramped atmosphere. The air had not been depleted. There were no telltale signs that I had been visited by an alien like I had seen in the movies.

I returned to my chair and stared blankly at the concrete wall in front of me. What had just happened to me? Who or what was that man?

Was he human or a demon? Why was he sent to me, and who sent him?

Was he an angel of darkness imitating an angel of the light?

Would these questions be answered later on, or was I to always question this experience?

Chapter Two

STOPPING FOR A HAMBURGER

I had no choice but to put my recent exchanges behind me and move on.

Getting that unusual visit from the white-haired man out of my mind wasn't easy, though. No matter how many times I relived that encounter, I couldn't come up with any answers. I decided not to tell anyone. After all, what would I say?

I also came to the conclusion that moving to California was not in my children's best interests. I called my ex-husband and gave him the news.

For now, I chose to live in the present and take my children out to Krystal's hamburger drive-in eatery for a rare treat. Of course, they were excited, and I didn't have to make the suggestion twice to them.

DeAnna sat in the front seat, and the boys stood in the back. In the early 70s, then, seatbelts weren't required.

I pulled into an empty parking stall. After putting my car in park and switching off the motor, I rested my hands on the steering wheel and glanced around.

The early summer evening had a playful feel to it. My children DeAnna, Ricky, and Scotty were on their best behavior since mentioning that we may go to Krystal's. As a single mother on a budget, they appreciated this rare treat.

After gathering their hamburger orders, I reached for the phone receiver on the call box to place our orders. I had to lean slightly out of my driver's window so that I could reach it. When I did, my eyes locked with a blonde guy parked two stalls over.

I quickly freed my eyes and placed our orders. Since DeAnna was the older sister, she instructed her brothers what to do when their food arrived. I laughed to myself. I knew the boys would ignore her, but I certainly enjoyed listening to the dialogue going on between them.

I begin to reminisce about a time several years earlier, a time my mother referred to as "B.C.," meaning *before children*. Back then, my friends and I used to cruise Main Street. I thought, *how many times had I ridden through this Krystal's and cruised through the other drive-ins on the main strip?*

The guys used it as a platform to show off their cars as they passed by, their radios blaring to "Surf City," "Blue Velvet," or "Sugar Shack." That setting was very similar to that of the movie *American Graffiti*.

I cherished those memories. However, I chose to look ahead and not spend too much time looking in the rear-view mirror.

"Here come the hamburgers!" DeAnna proclaimed, breaking into my trip down Memory Lane.

I watched the carhop as she approached us and then carefully placed the silver aluminum tray on the car's door. I handed her the money, including a tip. She smiled. As she walked away, I wondered what it would be like to be a curb girl. It appeared to be a fun job.

While passing out the hamburgers, fries, and cokes, I used the universal language that all mothers use when eating with small children: "Be careful. Sit down and try not to spill anything. Keep your napkin close to you."

I was enjoying this time with my children. At that moment, I was completely at ease, with nothing to distract me from this summer night. Life was good.

I had moved in with my grandmother. After my grandfather died, it was a good arrangement for both of us. The kids kept her spirits lifted, not to mention it was a financial plus for me.

Entering My Car without Permission

After finishing our meal, I took the order phone to request a pick-up. Again, my eyes were in a straight line with the blonde guy. He was still staring at me. I also noticed that the other person sitting in the car with him was a Hispanic guy with a large afro.

"Hey, are those children yours?" the blonde guy yelled.

His question caught me off guard. I quickly responded, "Yes."

Then he followed with another question I considered inappropriate. "Hey, are you married?"

"Well, yes, kind of, sort of." My answer jumped out of my mouth like someone else had spoken.

What had I just said? I had always ignored cat whistles and yells and thought that any woman who responded to them was shallow. So then, who had responded to this blonde-headed guy? Not me. To do so would have been strictly against my upbringing, and I wasn't shallow. Nevertheless, I came to the shameful realization that it was indeed I who had spoken.

I could feel the eyes and ears from those in the surrounding cars waiting to see how this conversation was going to progress. Their interest reminded me of a lioness crouching, waiting, and watching for her prey.

I stared in disbelief as he approached my car. I wanted to turn the ignition on and slam my car into reverse, but that would have brought a lot of unwanted attention on myself, especially if I drove off with an aluminum tray full of empty glasses still attached to my car.

He walked around to the passenger's side door. DeAnna stood in the front seat, but she quickly jumped in the back. The blonde guy now had his head partially in the car window.

He was very handsome with clean and glossy shoulder-length blonde hair, blue-green eyes with extremely long lashes, and a wide smile with straight teeth. He wore only blue jeans, which showed off his well-built body.

"Momma, don't let him in!" exclaimed DeAnna.

Before I could speak, he tried to open the passenger's door, but it wouldn't open. Undeterred, he climbed through the window with ease.

"Hey, my name is Rick. Are these kids yours?" he asked, half laughing.

"Yes, they are." I tried to sound in control and stern.

"Are you married? Is your husband in the service?" He continued without waiting for me to answer. "You're even better-looking close up."

"No, I'm not married," I replied. I tried to recapture some composure so that I could provide some sort of intelligent response to this person who had just entered my car without permission.

He continued to fire questions at me. "Where do you live?"

Surprisingly, I continued to answer them. I also found out things about him too. I discovered that we lived close to each other.

He asked for my phone number, and I found myself giving it to him. He climbed back out through the window and smiled. "I'll call you." With those words, he was off, heading toward his car.

By that time, the carhop came and removed the aluminum tray. I put the car in reverse, wondering all the while what that was all about.

The car ride back to Grandma's house was quiet, which was unusual with three small kids. DeAnna took her place as the big sister, jumping back over to take her rightful place in the front. Ricky and Scotty still stood tall in the backseat. It was like nothing out of the ordinary had just happened.

After putting the kids to bed that night, I settled into my own bed. Waiting for sleep to take over, my mind kept rehearsing the evening's events. Should I have said that or should I have said this? Regardless, I couldn't change any word or sentence I had said to the blonde stranger.

I tossed and turned for hours, wondering if morning would ever come.

Chapter Three

THE BAND

Time had passed since the Krystal's incident, and I eventually forgot about the blonde guy.

Life had settled into a routine. I continued working at my job at the airport, and the kids and I had adjusted well at Grandma's house.

Then, out of the blue, an interesting and unexpected twist of fate occurred. While getting the kids ready for bed one evening, my grandmother called for me.

"Marsha, telephone."

"Okay. I'll take it in the bedroom." I made my way to my room.

"Hello," I said. Silence.

I repeated, "Hello?"

Still no answer. I hung up the phone. I took a few steps, and it rung again.

"Hello," I answered, waiting for the other party to answer.

I then heard a male voice ask, "Is your husband at home?"

"You must have the wrong number." I hung up the phone again. I barely got turned around, and it rang again.

I thought that whoever was calling had to be redialing the wrong number. I picked up the receiver to answer it.

"Is this Marsha?"

"Who is this?" I asked.

"Is your husband at home?"

"I don't know you, and you obviously don't know me." Now I was irritated.

"Wait, wait. This is Rick. You met me at Krystal's."

"Why did you ask me if my husband was at home?"

"Well, I thought maybe you were married to a sailor, and he was home or something."

"I told you I was divorced. Do you usually call married women?"

He laughed, and I could hear people talking or laughing in the background.

I asked, "What do you want?"

"Do you want to come over and hear my band practice?"

"Your band?" I was surprised. I didn't realize he was a musician.

"Yes, I have a band."

I had never met anyone in a band, and I found his request interesting. This person had a mysterious appeal. Not only was he good-looking, but he was a lot different from the few dates I had been on. My adventurous and impulsive personality pulled at me to go.

I asked, "When are you practicing?"

"Tonight. We practice every Friday night. I know you want to come."

I should have said no. He was too sure of himself.

"Okay, after I put my kids to bed."

Did I say that? I guess I did and admittedly, I was curious about him. Listening to the band was just a side benefit.

I took my time putting the children to bed that night. With each passing minute, I contemplated what the night may bring.

Getting three little ones to bed sometimes can be an experience in itself. But most of the time they were very good, with a few exceptions.

This Friday night was no different. As the youngest, Scotty crawled into bed first. Ricky slept in the middle, and then DeAnna climbed into bed last.

I gave each of my children a goodnight kiss before pulling a thin sheet over them. I adjusted the oscillating fan at the foot of the bed to blow equally on all three.

I looked out the open bedroom window and saw a cool breeze sway Grandma's azaleas. The smell of summer lingered through the window screen.

The kids were clean, fed, and happy. I was happy as well.

"Goodnight. Sweet dreams," I whispered as I shut the bedroom door behind me.

"Grandma," I said quietly, not to disturb her too much while she watched *Hogan's Heroes* on the television. "I'm going out for a while. The kids are down for the night."

She turned to face me. "Okay. Be careful." She then went back to watching her show.

Guitars and Amps

The summer night was luring and enticing. It offered adventure with a touch of mystery, creating a perfect set up for something, but I wasn't sure what.

I drove slowly just to reflect back on the night I first met Rick. I had to admit, he intrigued me...or should I say mystified me?

As I parked my car, I felt an excitement sweep through me. The summer night breeze brought out a childlike nostalgia I hadn't felt in years.

Rick spotted me getting out of my car and approached me. His long blonde hair was wet with sweat. Again, his attire consisted of a pair of jeans only. Not only did he not wear a shirt this time, but he was barefoot. His smile was contagious, and I couldn't help but smile back.

The small house was full of people. I followed him into the living room where several girls and guys sat on the couch. Others stood in the hallway and dining area.

A light illuminated the hallway. However, a hanging light of purple grapes made up the only light in the living room.

I noticed that the grapes made a reflection on the dining room window. I wondered if this was a "hippie" house. I felt out of place. I was either way too old, or I was completely out of my element. I had stepped into a world entirely different from my own. Yes, I had smoked pot before, but this was a whole different scene. How would I fit in here?

Rick motioned for me sit down in one of the living room chairs. He walked outside before returning with two guys. I recognized one of them as the Hispanic guy from Rick's car. The other guy was short with red hair that matched the Hispanic guy's afro.

Rick and the red-headed guy picked up their guitars and tuned them. The Hispanic guy sat close to me with a set of bongo drums in his lap.

"One, two, three," Rick counted, and they began playing.

I didn't recognize the song. I sat and listened as the music from the amps filled every inch of the house and spilled over to the outside.

In the hall, I could see the silhouettes of faces and bodies swaying to the music. Even though I heard Rick singing, the only thing on my mind was what I was doing here. Now I really felt out of place. I wasn't ready for this unfamiliar world. I had decided that I would graciously bow out after this song and return to the safety and sanity of my life back at Grandma's.

The purple grapes turned with the music. They seemed to dance with the rhythm of the guitar. I watched their reflection on the window pane and tried to count their turns. My eyes then fell back on Rick, still playing his bass. His head bobbed up and down as if saying yes, yes. He was into the music, not just playing it. He seemed to be one with his instrument, and both were one with the music. I had never seen this happen.

The song ended, and the silhouettes clapped and whistled. I joined in too.

I thought, *Good. I'll just politely excuse myself now.*

The band immediately began to play another song. I felt as if I was sitting in the front row of a concert.

The amps pound out another unfamiliar song. My eyes diverted back to the hanging light, and I again counted the turns of the purple grapes.

The human silhouettes swayed, and some girls passed around a marijuana cigarette in the hallway. I could smell the sweet odor exude from the burning joint. It drifted into the atmosphere to mix with the night's aroma that had mysteriously drawn me.

Logic dictated that I should leave, but my body decided to stay. After several songs, the band stopped. So, did the purple grapes. My mind didn't stop, though. I wished the purple grapes had not stopped either, because they had visually entertained me.

I now felt as if I had entered a bizarre yet wonderful new place both enticing and frightening at the same time.

Rick put his guitar in its case. "Come on, Marsha," he said, motioning for me to join him.

I walked behind him as we went outside into the summer night. He grabbed my hand as if doing so was normal. I became caught up in a strange and unfamiliar mood. I felt drawn to him in a peculiar, uncontrollable way. It wasn't just his good looks or carefree-yet-in-control spirit. There was more, but I just couldn't put my finger on what.

Rick led me away from the house. He let go of my hand, and we walked down the street side by side.

He reached into the front pocket of his jeans. He pulled out a wrinkled joint, lit it, and passed it to me. I took a toke and passed it back. After smoking the joint, we headed back to the house.

He talked a lot, never once giving me the opportunity to respond. Upon our return to the house, I wanted to both stay and leave. What had I walked into?

Finally, I managed to tell him I was leaving. He followed me as I headed to my car.

When I reached for the door handle, he stood close behind me. I could feel his body almost touching mine.

I was so unsure of the situation in which I had placed myself. It was like two different personalities had taken residence within me.

I turned to face him. He placed both hands on top of my car and pinned me between them. Our bodies were just inches away from each other, but never touched.

"Ah, Rick, this has been interesting, and thanks for sharing the joint," I heard myself saying. "Well, see ya'll sometime."

"Yeah. I'll see you again." His eyes twinkled.

Yes, he did see me again. And again. And again.

Six months later, we were married.

Chapter Four

THE TRIP

What had I gotten myself into?

On one hand, I was in love with a man who seemed to be my best friend. Yet as the days passed, it felt like I was sleeping with a stranger.

At times, I thought the sun rose and set in him. At other times, I thought the wind had blown its cold dry breath of death upon me.

I loved how Rick was blessed with the abilities to play multiple instruments and compose songs. However, his genius came with a price; a temperament that was ever-changing and always unpredictable. That was the side of him I came to fear.

I found myself lost in a new world. Rick had, slowly and methodically, molded me into what he wanted me to be. I wasn't aware of it at the time, though. It wasn't until later when I learned how words are very powerful tools, used to shape or reshape someone's spirit.

I became comfortable with his rock 'n roll world. Being around creative people opened my mind up to thoughts that I had never entertained. I left behind the familiar and embraced the unknown.

Admittedly, those years were marked with fun, excitement, and intrigue while simultaneously laced with the ingredients of poison that led to pain, disappointment, and distrust. The combination caused me to question who I was. Had my perceptions changed? I don't think words can describe what went through my mind. I had never experienced both verbal and physical abuse to this extent. I had never been exposed to the kind of life I was now living. To reiterate, my dream was to be a wife and a mother and enjoy a quiet, simple life.

Confusion and pain became my constant companions; they accompanied me everywhere. I knew in order to survive, I had to leave. First, I needed to make some good money, and fast. So, I found myself bartending.

Prior to this job, I believed women who worked in clubs didn't have good character. But as a result of working in this environment, I came to form a much different opinion. These women were smart, intelligent, kind, and trustworthy. They possessed high moral values, at least most of them. As with every job, there were exceptions to the rule, and I was about to find that out firsthand.

In my line of work, I met many different types of people. Truth became fuzzy at times, so discernment was needed. I wasn't naïve, but I naturally always believed the best in people.

I shared some of my personal life with Kathy, one of the bartenders at the club. I assumed she was different from me because of her culture. I grew up in the South, whereas she had moved here from the west coast.

Sometimes all six bartenders got high while working. One Saturday night while tending bar, my high allowed me to feel quite happy. I was having a good time with my customers and the waitresses.

Our club always had live bands and stayed packed. Kathy came all the way down to my end of the bar.

Leaning in, she whispered in my ear, "You're a good person, but the last good person I knew is dead now."

I was in the middle of mixing drinks. My mind heard those words, but I couldn't process them at the time. They entered my brain and swirled around, but they never found a resting place.

At the end of the night while we were closing, I thought about what she had said to me. For some strange reason, I kept it to myself.

Into the Depths of Hell

Several weeks went by. I never brought up to her what she said to me that night.

In the meantime, I made the decision to leave Rick. I wanted to move to Miami because I was familiar with it from spending summers with relatives who lived there. It had become my second home.

I discussed my ideas with some of the bartenders. Kathy and I put together a plan of action, and Eric, one of the busboys, decided to come with us. I made arrangements for DeAnna, Ricky, and Scotty to stay with my sister for at least two weeks. I knew it would take that long to get settled.

Something had taken control of me. I had a new type of confidence in this adventure, which made me that more determined to go through with my decision.

This wasn't the first time I had left Rick. Before, I always returned, hoping and praying for change. He held a strange magnetism that kept drawing me to him. We had an unhealthy relationship, and thus an unhealthy marriage.

During those previous attempts to leave, I had to sneak away because I feared for my safety. Up until then, I didn't have the guts to face him and say, "Hey, guess what. I'm leaving you, and there's nothing you can do about it."

I believed doing so would have been suicide. Regardless of our bizarre attraction to each other, I couldn't stay with him. This time, I wouldn't be leaving in a hasty escape; this time I had a plan.

Now that my newly discovered confidence had kicked in, I told Rick exactly what I was going to do. He was upset and hurt, but not violent as I had expected. We even made love before I left, which shocked me.

So, Kathy, Eric, and I marched forward with our plan to move to Miami.

The night before we were to leave, I stayed with some of my girlfriends who lived at the beach. They each had a boyfriend, and I felt like a fifth wheel. One of the girls went to the store and came back with a tall stranger with long blonde hair. We hit it off right from the start. I called him "Sunshine."

Sunshine and I decided to walk on the beach. The night air was refreshing with the wind blowing over the ocean. We sat on the sand dune and lit a joint, neither of us speaking. We just watched the dark waves break against the rocks, and the night sky blend into the sea.

Finally, I asked him, "Where are you from, and where are you going?"

He looked at me with kindness, but his voice was serious. "Nowhere and headed somewhere."

I stared at the ocean, fully understanding those words.

I told Sunshine about my trip and the reason for it. I asked, "Would Miami be somewhere you may want to go?"

He said, "Yes, I'll come with you."

Asking him, a complete stranger, may have seemed strange, but that was where my mind was at that time.

The next morning, I drove to Kathy's house liked we had planned.

I handed her the keys to my car and climbed in the backseat, determined to enjoy this trip and not shoulder the responsibility of getting us to our destination. Sunshine climbed in the back with me.

So, we all left for the adventure of my lifetime.

Just for the fun of it, we decided to make a quick stop at Disney World along the way. At this time, I felt a freedom that I hadn't experienced since I was seventeen.

The first night of our journey, we rented a motel room. We then watched the movie *Deliverance*. The next day, we drove to Kissimmee to see some of Kathy's friends.

I felt safe as we drove through her friends' quiet neighborhood. It had a warm, friendly feel. I noted the sidewalks that outlined the neatly manicured lawns.

We pulled into a driveway of a white concrete-block house that blended in well with the other homes. Several orange trees stood in the front yard. The whole setting brought back memories of my summers in Miami.

Kathy knocked on the dark-blue front door as the three of us waited in the car. She went in, and a few minutes later, she motioned for us to come in too.

When I entered the house, I felt the same way as when I first went to hear Rick and his band play.

We settled in, and quick introductions were made, but I knew these people weren't that interested in us. I tried to start a conversation with one of the young girls, but she seemed distant. They didn't seem very friendly.

The guy who seemed to be in charge then asked if I would like to see something.

I thought, *Why not?*

He led me to a bedroom with a lock on the outside of the door, which he slipped a key into. I had a weird feeling about this.

I followed him into the room and he closed the door. Large posters hung on the walls. I looked at them closer and saw that they were really pictures of him and others standing in what looked like a desert. They held guns and rifles.

Some of the pictures depicted them standing with bandoleers criss-crossed over their chests. Some had large knives in their hands and were posing like soldiers training for war.

A large table sat in its center of the room. Several rifles, knives, and boxes of ammunition lay on top of it. Black curtains covered the single window.

He smiled at me. "What do you think of this?"

I smiled back, trying not to come across as too dumbfounded. Of course, I had never experienced seeing these kinds of things to this magnitude.

I said, "My first rifle was a Daisy BB gun that I got for Christmas when I was eight years old. Then my Grandpop taught me how to shoot a single-shot four-ten shotgun. For a girl, I could shoot fairly well, but my dad told me that if I shot an animal, I would have to eat it. So, I just shot at targets or cans."

He laughed.

After walking out of the room, I felt strange. I wanted to ask more questions but felt a check inside not do so.

That night, I slept on the floor next to Sunshine. I still wore the same clothes as when we arrived.

The next morning, we thanked our hosts and headed to Disney World. Kathy controlled most of the group's decisions, and that was fine with me. Eric was just there, a kind spirit who just wanted to have fun and get high. I noticed that Sunshine hardly spoke to either Kathy or Eric.

Before buying our tickets, we smoked a joint. I felt childlike with no worries.

Sunshine suggested we separate and meet back at the gate later in the day. Kathy agreed, but I knew she wasn't happy about it.

Sunshine spotted a guy and asked me to wait while he approached him. He came back and handed me a small piece of paper. I knew it contained LSD. I had taken acid before, although it had been a while.

I put the small paper in my mouth and swallowed it. In a few minutes, we both were enjoying this trip. The acid was a mellow type.

We went on rides and enjoyed climbing the Swiss Family Treehouse and watching the people. We laughed, smiled, and talked.

Later on, we sat down and shared a hot dog and Coke. I liked Sunshine. He was becoming my friend.

The time came to meet Kathy and Eric. We then headed into the parking lot to find our car.

I noticed Sunshine walking several steps behind Kathy and Eric. I slowed down to join him.

He looked at me, his gaze steady and grave. We were still high, but something deep in his eyes silently spoke to me, like he was trying to convey an important message to me.

He slowed down more. I fell in step beside him.

"Marsha," he said, not in a whisper but a low tone that I hadn't heard him use before.

He then stopped and faced me. His blue eyes were dilated due to the acid, but he was in complete control. "Your friends are evil."

The words floated out of his mouth, carrying blackness with them as they echoed through me. I tried to ignore them, but the ominous feeling inside of me validated his words.

The sun was going down, and the sky displayed a beautiful mix of colors, primary dark blues with hints of golden rays peeking out. There was a chill in the air, but it didn't feel cold. I pulled my poncho up on my shoulders and continued to walk.

We headed south. My good high was about to turn into a very bad low. I can't say how far we drove, but everything turned black. When I say "everything," I mean *everything*.

It was like someone had put a black blindfold on me. My eyes were open, but the darkness was all I could see and feel. I only remember bits and pieces of that night. Sunshine seemed to be there, but even though I couldn't see him, I felt his presence.

He was right. Kathy and Eric were evil, especially Kathy. I could feel the evil emanating from her.

I felt like the evil had swallowed me up, and it was terrifying. At times, I grasped a speck of reality, but that was short-lived. I descended into a very dark, cold place. Words can't describe where I went. Instinctively, I knew I had, literally, been transported to that horrific place called hell.

Terror, fright, and complete darkness could only begin to relay the truth of the hell I experienced. I was encapsulated by the horror of the unknown and whether or not I was doomed to remain in this terrible place. I didn't see anything, hear anything, or smell anything, but I felt the pure evil of existing there. Beyond that, it can't be compared to any horror here on Earth. All I could do was scream, "Jesus, Jesus, Jesus!"

He must have heard my call because I heard Him say to me, "My harvest is plenty, and my laborers are few. You will work for me."

All I could say was "Yes!" I'm not sure if my mouth vocalized my response or if my spirit did.

I remained in a supernatural realm, and I had no contact with the earthly plane. Then, little by little, the darkness seemed to subside. By the time my physical eyes begin to see light, I understood more clearly how darkness was ever-present in this world.

My physical eyes slowly adjusted to the light. Glancing around my environment, I realized all four of us were now in a motel room that looked like a tornado had blown through it. I wondered if I had caused the destruction while trying to get away from evil.

Also, someone had changed my clothes, even down to my underwear. I wondered why and who was responsible.

Sunshine took me by the hand and led me out of the motel room. I knew that twenty-four hellish hours had passed since entering my supernatural experience because it was morning again.

"Marsha," he said softly, "we're in Miami now, but I need to bring you to a safe place away from Kathy. She is evil."

I wasn't sure about anything or anyone. What was real? For some reason, I trusted this stranger whom I had spent every minute with during the last three days.

"I want to call my aunt," I said, still trying to process everything.

I spotted a payphone and pointed to it. Sunshine grabbed my hand and gently pulled me in that direction. He pulled two quarters from front pocket and dropped them into the phone's coin slot.

"Hello, Marsha!" my aunt said when she realized it was me.

At first, she sounded worried, but after a couple of minutes of explaining, I heard the relief in her voice.

I wasn't sure where I was, but knew I was close to an airport. Sunshine took the phone and gave her a better description of our location. She gave Sunshine the directions to her house and threatened to call the police on him if I wasn't there within the hour.

Sunshine and I then returned to the motel room. When we entered, I saw Kathy and Eric. The eerie atmosphere lingered throughout like a thick fog. No one spoke. It was as if an unwritten law of silence was being enforced between all four of us.

We packed up the car and got in. Up until then, Kathy had driven with Eric in the front seat and Sunshine and me in the back. This time, Sunshine sat in the driver's seat, and I did too. Kathy and Eric sat in the back.

The rule of silence continued unbroken during the car ride. Sunshine skillfully guided the car to my aunt's house as if he had a map inside his head.

When we all got out of the car, Kathy and Eric quickly grabbed their backpacks and headed off down the sidewalk without a word. Sunshine walked me to the door of the house carrying my backpack.

He looked down at me, his eyes speaking volumes of kindness and understanding as he stroked my long, straight dark hair. He never said a word. He then turned around, and I watched his tall, lanky body walk away. That was the last time I ever say him.

I entered my aunt's house, still unsure of everything and everyone.

Chapter Five

THE BITES

I hoped I would be able to explain this next experience. Like my experience in hell, describing what went on in the unseen realm that was more real to me than the one in which we live. Two powerful forces warred against each other in the battleground of my mind. I didn't enlist in this battle, but because of its chosen terrain, I was inadvertently pulled into this fight. It turned out to be the fight of my life, and it forced me to choose sides, even though I hadn't been trained for it and didn't understand the rules of engagement.

What had possessed me? Somewhere in this journey while I was in that supernatural realm, a spirit told me I had been killed in a car wreck, and I had to be good in order to get to heaven.

The only truth I knew was that Jesus had spoken to me. I knew this fact even though I hadn't been in church in years and wasn't looking for Him. Until someone encounters Him, I can't expect anyone to understand this revelation I received. I wanted Jesus, and I was determined that He would be the only One I would trust.

I wasn't sure if I was dead or if my experience was a part of death. What raged in me left me completely unprepared I had been jerked into a world of wickedness and couldn't even trust my own thoughts.

For the most part, I kept trying to hold on to the Marsha I remembered. Thank God for my Aunt Eden Ruth. She had rescued me, and Uncle Woodrow took my bizarre actions in stride.

After arriving at her house that day, she put me in the shower, washed my hair, and put clean clothes on me.

Ever since that horrid experience, I could sense the supernatural realm. I knew good and evil were everywhere.

I had taken refuge in the bedroom. Not only were some of my actions peculiar, but I stayed in a distant realm, an unseen world that made no sense to an outsider. That place became my reality, but unfortunately visitors were denied access. Even my cousin Dale, a nurse, couldn't communicate with me. I remained detached from everyone.

Since no one in my family had heard from me in three days, they were relieved to hear that I was now at my aunt's house. I later learned they had notified the police. My mother and Rick immediately left Jacksonville, making the six-hour drive to Miami to get me.

When they arrived, they came in my bedroom. Rick's presence threw me into a rage. I tried to hurt him any way I could. I hit him with my fist and I clawed at his face. I pulled his long hair and ripped his shirt.

I sensed evil all around him. Of course, my ninety-eight-pound frame was no match for his two hundred twenty-pound body. Nevertheless, this kind of behavior was way out of character for me.

They brought DeAnna with them, so I grabbed her and held her against me. Protecting her was my goal. I would have given my life for her. Evil would not have my daughter.

Many other strange things happened. These unseen spirits attacked me viciously, and the battleground was my mind.

They spoke to me from within, saying, "Remember you are dead, and no one is real, not your daughter or your mother. You can walk through walls and fly because nothing in the material world obstructs you. Just come to the light."

That night, as my cousin Dale was talking with me, my actions became too strange and unpredictable. I was freaking everyone out. They decided I needed medical attention, so we headed to the hospital.

Rick and I sat in the backseat with DeAnna, and I refused to let go of my daughter. When we got to the emergency room at Jackson Memorial in Miami, Rick carried me inside. I tried to resist by fighting him, but to no avail. The nurses immediately put me in a secluded room, one only the doctor and nurses could enter.

I finally began to calm down. The doctor recommended that I be admitted to the hospital and placed in the mental ward. For some reason Rick refused that, so we returned to my aunt's house. No one could understand me or how to reach me. They had no idea what to do. Finally, I was so exhausted that my body collapsed.

I made sure DeAnna slept beside me in one of the twin beds. Rick slept on the other one.

During that night, I left my body. I felt myself flying out the window and into the clouds. The sensation was so amazing, and I didn't sense any evil. When I returned to my body, I felt an evil presence land on top of me.

Upon waking the next morning, I was suspicious about everything, although I felt more in control than before. I knew the invisible presence still hovered around me, wanting to hurt me, so having my family around made me feel safer.

At the time, I thought I controlled the forces of good and evil. I went to the bathroom and stared into the large mirror over the sink. On my shoulder were two bite marks. I thought they couldn't be real. Surely the invisible realm hadn't crossed over to the physical realm?

When I touched my fingers to those marks, I could feel them. I called my mother in to verify they were actually in the physical realm because my mind was still unclear as to which one I was in.

I asked, "How did I get these?"

"Marsha, I don't know. Last night was a very bad night...for all of us." The fear and terror that filled her eyes said more than words. Even though her demeanor remained calm, I sensed she was struggling with this undeniable physical evidence before her eyes.

I imagined what she had just experienced exhausted her as well, which probably played a part in her inability to handle the thought of her baby daughter being hurt in this way.

"Where is Rick?" I asked, angry. "Did he bite me?"

I left the bathroom and found Rick, Aunt Eden Ruth, Uncle Woodrow, and DeAnna in the kitchen. All looked very worn and tired. I showed them the bites. They all asked how I got them.

"No one bit you, Marsha," Rick said. "You're the one who attacked me."

He got up and left. A few moments later, he came back carrying his shirt. Its tattered condition all but said that I had ripped it off him. It was proof of what I had done.

I asked, "I did that?" I couldn't believe I had actually ripped off his shirt. I became more confused. The reasons for my actions weren't clear. I was still in a different realm.

The events of last night began to slowly spin around in my memory.

Rick repeated, "No one bit you, Marsha."

I asked, "Then how did these teeth marks get on me?"

"Mamma," DeAnna spoke. Her voice was of a nine-year-old child, but what she was about to say was something no nine-year-old child should have seen. "Last night, a gold wolf head came out of the sky through the window and landed on your head. It was so evil. It scared me so much that it sucked the breath out of me. I didn't think I could breathe."

No one said a word. After that, I again looked at the teeth marks. Their origin was definitely not human.

Back to the Scene of the Crime

That afternoon, my friend Mary came over. We had been friends since the age of ten.

We discussed the motel where I stayed, and I told them about the condition of the room when I woke up. I needed to make sure I hadn't imagined everything. I had to verify the reality of what I had faced that previous night, the evil that tried to destroy me, and my desperate attempts to get away. I believed the condition of that room would confirm to everyone, including me that I had dealt with forces that were not part of this world.

Dale and Mary both agreed that we should try to find the motel, so I described the area as best I could. I remembered a canal, boats tied up to a dock, and the sound of low-flying airplanes. I also remembered the color of the building.

About an hour later, Dale, Mary, Rick, and I located the motel. The manager gladly let us into the room. The room was a disaster. Curtains had been torn from the rods. The bed linens were scattered on the floor. I tried to imagine what had happened to me. Only God knew the truth. I only knew that I walked out of that motel twenty-four hours ago with my physical body intact; my mind, however, was a different story.

My exit from the motel had been hasty, I had wanted to get away from evil, yet it seemed to follow me. I was fighting against something, though I didn't really know what. I was engaged in a battle with an unknown force for my sanity and for my life. After all, those demonic spirits were trying to convince me that I had been killed in a car wreck.

I found out later that Kathy was a witch, and she was part of a coven out west. She mentioned one time that she had met some of Charles Manson's followers but never elaborated on it. Rick believed she wanted to sacrifice me or use me in a satanic ritual. I wasn't sure if that was true what I do know is that whatever I had experienced was evil and it had no mercy, hell is very real.

Chapter Six

THE RETURN

The next morning, we drove back to Jacksonville. Fortunately, nothing had changed in my apartment since my trip to Miami ended.

I cherished familiarity more so than ever, but I didn't know if I would ever fully return to it. The Marsha I knew all my life was gone.

My daily routine did return, though. DeAnna, Ricky, and Scotty were my lifelines. I loved being their mother, and they were stabilizers for me.

Rick took a construction job. With him working all day and the kids in school, I was left alone. Even though I had left the evil presence behind in Miami, it still pursued me, but so was the Greater One. He had spoken to me and was also pursuing me.

When I was younger, I went to church with my grandparents and had a deep reverence for God. I wanted so much to meet Jesus; the real Jesus. I had to know beyond a shadow of a doubt that Jesus was the One who had spoken with such authority and rescued me from depths of hell.

I was hungry for Him and desperate to get to know Him. A young Christian girl named Sandy, in our apartment complex gave me Oral Roberts' magazines. I had never heard of Oral Roberts, but I enjoyed reading his magazines anyway.

I also had a Bible and read it daily. After dropping the kids off at school, I drove to a small park with a pond, sat barefoot under a tree, lit a joint, and read. I was led to read Ephesians, Galatians, and the other epistles of Paul for the first time. I could feel God's love flowing into me as I read.

On days when I was alone in the apartment, those spirits manifested as dark shadows on the wall and spoke to me. Even though I didn't hear them audibly, they left very clear impressions in my mind. They reminded me that I was killed in the car wreck, and for me to get to heaven, I had to be good. They continually said things that sounded correct and religious.

Still, I wanted so much to meet Jesus, the real One. The spirits kept trying to convince me that I was dead and in a holding place and that none of this was real. They kept telling me that I was trying to relive my life here on earth and that I must let go of my kids, and Rick, to get to heaven. I still was torn between two worlds of the unseen and the seen. Unfortunately, the unseen world was more real to me.

This day was darker than usual. The atmosphere around me seemed mixed with confusion and guilt. All I could think about was that I had to be good to go to heaven. Thoughts that I needed to be truthful and honest flooded the logical side of my brain.

I did have a secret, though, a dark secret that I hadn't told anyone. I was ashamed but not regretful. How could that be? I had slept with Sunshine on my trip to Miami.

Before, I had always prided myself for not sleeping around, even after my divorce. I had many opportunities to do so during the two years I was single, but I refused the offers. Infidelity was the one thing I knew I would have to own up to. The voices agreed with me. I felt this was the key that would assure my admittance to heaven. The voices again agreed with me.

That night I put the kids to bed as usual. One of our friends stopped by and sat on the couch with me while I read Oral Roberts' magazine.

One of Rick's musician friends had come by too, and they were having a conversation about music. The spirits spoke louder than usual that night. I could see their dark shadows lurking on the walls, manifesting by changing shapes and keeping me in suspense at what they were doing.

After our friends left, I had an impression pounding deep within me that I would be in heaven tonight. First, though, it caused me to believe that I needed to tell Rick about my adultery against him.

I sensed it say, "You have been good. Now is your opportunity to see Jesus."

My heart was relieved. I felt no fear. I trusted this voice within me.

I stood up from the couch and walked toward Rick, who was coming out of the kitchen.

I put my arms around him. His blue-green eyes stared down at me.

My voice was happy and confident. "Rick, I have something I need to tell you. Remember the guy, the hitchhiker that I told you about named Sunshine? I slept with him."

He immediately dropped to his knees in front of me. I reached down and patted his back, telling him it was okay. I then said, "Now I'm going to heaven. Everything will be alright. I get to go to heaven."

Rick yelled as he stood up, "God told me to kill the bitch!"

With the force of a professional boxer, his fist slammed into my face and all went black. I'm not sure how long I was unconscious, but when I came to, Rick had carried me to our bedroom and laid me on the bed.

He stood in the doorway of the bedroom. Behind him was a large form of something very bright.

Rick said, "Marsha, we have to go to the hospital."

He then picked me up and carried me to the car. His strong arms made me feel safe. Strangely, I felt no pain.

Rick drove to our babysitter's house a couple of blocks away to ask her to watch the kids so that he could take me to the hospital. I was thankful that the kids had stayed asleep and not been disturbed by what had taken place.

The babysitter climbed into the backseat of the car. Her eyes were wide, and her eyebrows were furrowed.

I think my very appearance must have frightened her.

Chapter Seven

DO YOU KNOW JESUS?

After watching the babysitter go inside our apartment, Rick drove me to the emergency room. The darkness outside of the car window was nothing compared to the darkness inside the car.

Rick drove directly up to the emergency entrance. He picked me up right from the passenger seat. I thought, *why is he carrying me? I can walk.*

The emergency room doors swing open as if someone had waved a magic wand, and Rick carried me to the triage desk.

The nurse glanced up at me, and I saw the color drain from her face. Why were people looking at me so weirdly?

Immediately, the nurse took the wheelchair next to her desk and pushed it to Rick. I felt his strong arms releasing their hold on me as he lowered me into it.

The nurse led Rick through the double doors into the exam area and to the first empty bed. She then helped me out of the wheelchair and onto the hard vinyl mattress covered by a thin white sheet.

The nurse was kind but very professional, gently putting the blood pressure cuff around my arm. She took my pressure before pulling the green curtain that separated the patients' beds. Rick followed her out. I was left alone in my tiny, green-curtained compartment.

Although I had been knocked unconscious, I was very much awake now. Still, I felt alienated to my surroundings. I knew I was in the emergency room, with its intermingling medicinal and cleaning solution smells and its unappealing drab interior. I could hardly stand the overhead glaring fluorescent light.

I took everything in the doctors, the nurses, and the sick people who were also in their own green-curtained tents. I couldn't see them, but I could hear their voices. I heard Rick tell the nurse what had happened to me. Still, I wasn't sure what was real or what was counterfeit. At this point I was not going to trust anyone.

The curtain opened, and a doctor walked in. "Mrs. Yarbrough, I'm going to start an IV and send you for X-rays," he said.

I sat up. He wanted me to lie down.

I said, "I don't want to lie down. I feel better sitting up."

I needed to be in control. Lying down, I felt vulnerable.

He left, and I remained sitting up with my legs dangling over the bed. A nurse came in to start the IV. Behind her walked Rick and two policemen.

One of the police officers asked, "Do you know why you're in the ER? Your husband admitted to hitting you."

I answered, "Yes, I know, and yes, Rick hit me."

The other officer asked, "Do you want to press charges against your husband?"

"Of course not," I replied. "I'm on my way to heaven. Do you know Jesus?"

They stared at me for a second before walking out of the room, Rick right behind them.

The nurse continued setting up the IV. She wore a genuine smile, and her touch felt gentle, but she never spoke to me.

The curtain opened again, and another doctor entered. He told me his name and that he was a psychiatrist.

He asked, "Marsha, do you know why you're here?"

I didn't answer. His questions kept coming, reminding me of the first time Rick entered my life, climbing shirtless into my car. I thought about how Rick fired question after question at me. Before I could answer one question, he'd ask me another one. Why did my mind bring that up?

"Do you know the president's name? Do you know your children's names? Do you know your mother's name?"

I thought, *Is this man real or has the devil sent him to me? Did he think he could trick me and stop me from meeting Jesus?*

"Do you know Jesus?" I fired back at him. I had determined that I would not answer anyone who couldn't tell me they knew Jesus.

The psychiatrist wrote something on his clipboard and left. I hadn't answered any of his questions. I, of course, knew the answers.

After I had X-rays taken of my head and face, the hospital porter rolled me to the intensive care unit. All the rooms in that area had open doors and windows that let you see everything and everyone. My room sat across from the nurse's station.

While one of the nurses was taking my vital signs, she asked, "Do you know you're in the hospital?"

I asked, "Do you know Jesus?"

She smiled but didn't answer.

The dark spirits were still very active, and I was waiting to go to heaven. I still wondered that if this was death, how much longer I had to wait to get to heaven. I had been good, and I had confessed my sins.

I could still see into the unseen realm and the spirit realm continued to reveal itself to me. I watched the shadows of death and pain swirl around like a fog as it went from patient to patient in the intensive care unit. Strange as all of this may sound, I was unafraid. I was so focused on meeting Jesus.

I had begun this journey, and no one or nothing was going to stop me from being with Jesus. I had experienced hell that terrorized me with evil, a type of evil that can't be explained in any language. I knew Satan was real, and I knew Jesus was real.

The dawn's light crept slowly between the blinds of my hospital room. It became apparent to me that my journey to heaven had taken a detour. The intensive care unit looked a lot different from several hours earlier when it was immersed in darkness, enabling those shadows to roam freely. Once the light arrived, I couldn't see those spirits, but I knew they were still there.

I had not rested due to the activity of nurses taking my vitals every four hours and asking me questions. I still continued to answer their questions with my own: "Do you know Jesus?" No one gave me a yes or a no, just a smile. How do you read a smile? Some people smile when they're lying, and others smile when they have wrong motives. Smiles can represent anything, and anyone can wear one.

I watched the hustle and bustle of the morning shift change. Nurses smiled as they left, and fresh nurses came in for their duty.

Even amidst the comings and goings, I felt at peace. Something deep inside me was surrendering. I wasn't sure if I was exhausted from this fight or if I was getting a second wind for the next battle. Regardless, I embraced it.

One of the doctors I remembered from the ER came in with two more doctors. Again, they asked me who I was. Did I know I was in the hospital?

I became very agitated being asked the same questions. I again asked them, "Do you know Jesus?" If they couldn't answer me, then why should I answer them? Was this some kind of test to find out if I qualified for heaven? I wasn't going to answer anyone who couldn't say YES, they knew Jesus.

I thought, *Doesn't anyone know Jesus?*

I knew all the answers to those questions they asked me. However, it scared me that no one who I had encountered in the last twenty-four hours knew Jesus or had even acknowledged that they had ever heard of Him. My peaceful feeling was short-lived. Now fear charged in on me like a war horse going to battle.

Had I not passed the test? Was I going to stay in the realm of the unknown? What was the next test? Would I ever be at peace again? Was this real or unreal? What about my DeAnna, Ricky, and Scotty?

I had felt the horror of hell with its cold darkness and evil presence that was so wicked. The only way to describe hell was isolation from God, which no one could fathom.

This was beginning to feel like hell, except things were clearer in the natural realm. Hell was in the unseen realm of the human body.

Two nurses informed me that they were transferring me to another hospital because I didn't have the right insurance.

I thought, *Okay now. I'm leaving here. I hope this is for my good. I was at their mercy.*

The Surgery

Morning was in full swing. Breakfast had arrived.

A young black girl entered my room with my tray. She set it on the table before rolling it to the side of my bed. She looked at me and then quickly looked away. I wondered what she saw. Before I could remove the lid covering my food, the nurse came in and told me I could have nothing to eat. She picked up my tray and took it away. I wasn't hungry anyway.

Not too much later, two young men came in with a gurney. With gentle hands, they placed me on it. They wheeled me out of intensive care and down the corridors. They had me sitting in an upright position, and I was thankful for that.

They rolled me out of the ER and into the back of a waiting ambulance. One of them stayed in the back with me. He was young and had a very kind demeanor.

Before the ambulance took off, I asked him, "Do you know Jesus?"

He answered me. "Yes ma'am. I go to First Baptist Church downtown."

My heart leaped, and fear left me. "Well, you can ride with me."

I arrived at the other hospital with my newfound friend. As they guided my gurney into this hospital, again through the ER, I held the young man's hand who knew Jesus. I felt safe for the first time in a long time. Someone had finally said he knew Jesus.

After I was moved from the gurney to the ER bed, peace again settled inside me. I was ready for my next stage of this trip. Everything seemed to take on a different light. The nurses seemed friendlier, and the atmosphere had changed.

They moved me from the ER into a private room. I had not talked to Rick or anyone else. I missed my children. My normal world, as I referred to it in my head, was somewhere out there. The abnormal world that I had grown used to was still inside of me, silent.

After the nurses settled me into my room, they set up my IV and told me that the doctor would be in soon. I thanked them. I hadn't spoken to anyone for more than twenty-four hours except for asking, "Do you know Jesus?" Now I was free to speak, and I wasn't afraid anymore.

They left me alone. For the first time I walked, pulling my IV with me to the sink. I had not been allowed to stand in the intensive care unit.

I wanted to wash my face. I turned the water on and let its warmth flow over my hands. I looked up at the mirror, thinking the face looking back at me was a monster. Again, fear gripped me.

I suddenly realized that the face I saw actually belonged to me. It was black and blue and distorted, and both sides of my jaw were swollen and drooping like they were resting too close to my shoulders. My eyes were the only feature I recognized, and that recognition brought calmness to me. Still, I felt no pain.

I just stared at this hideous face looking back at me, but deep inside, I was okay. My eyes peered through the swollen tissue, speaking to me like someone else had entered. I was not sure who that someone was. It wasn't the Marsha I had previously known. I knew everything was going to be different; good but different.

Four doctors came in to talk with me. One of them told me I was going to need surgery and asked if I had eaten anything. I told them no.

One of them read my chart and passed it to the man beside him. The first doctor asked, "Do you know your name?"

"Of course, I know my name. It's Marsha Dianne Young Yarbrough. I also know who the President is, and my children's names are DeAnna Lynn, Richard Jerome, and Robert Scott. I live in Jacksonville, Florida. I am in the hospital because I told my husband Rick that I had committed adultery, and he said the Lord told him to kill the bitch. I'm not crazy, nor am I on drugs. Now can I ask ya'll a question? Do you know Jesus?"

They all smiled, and again no one answered me. But at this point, I didn't care if they knew Jesus or not. I knew Him, and that was all that matter to me.

They informed me that I had a compound fracture of both sides of my jaw. My X rays showed that one of the bones was externally coming through my skin and contamination could cause infection. I needed immediate surgery, which was scheduled to begin within the next hour.

Even after seeing my hideous face and being told I needed immediate surgery, I felt as if someone had taken over, causing me to once more feel peaceful. I felt as if sweet dewdrops had gently kissed me all over, and security and safety had become my best friends. Those doctors could have told me almost anything, and it would have been okay with me. They had not given me any pain medicines, but I was engulfed in His peace.

The surgery lasted eight hours.

I woke to the doctor calling my name. "Marsha, Marsha, wake up."

I opened my eyes, but I couldn't open my mouth. A machine with a small tube was attached to the inside of my jaw, and it suctioned out my saliva.

"Marsha, because of the severity of the break we had to put three pins in your jaw. The type of trauma you suffered made this an uncommon fracture, so we had to wire your jaws together. Hopefully you won't have any complications.

"It usually takes about six weeks to heal, but in your case, it may take more. I believe we got it just in time to prevent infection. You're a very lucky girl to be alive." He softly patted my forehead.

I slipped back into that twilight sleep, still peaceful and happy. Was this the beginning of a new reality?

Chapter Eight

I FOUND HIM

Back in my hospital room, I wasn't sure what time it was. I knew it was daytime because the sun was shining through my window.

Waking up from an eight-hour operation to discover my jaw wired together was somewhat scary, especially for me. The anesthesia prevented me from fully comprehending what the doctor told me earlier in recovery. Now that it had worn off, reality hit hard. How was I going to communicate?

In less than six months, my world, as the saying goes, had been turned upside down. Now my task was to determine whether upside down was better than right side up. At this time, I needed to be still... literally.

After the second day, I figured out I could talk with my jaw wired, perhaps not well but clear enough for someone to understand. I felt like a ventriloquist, all I needed was a dummy on my arm. I had to sip broth and other liquids through a small straw after placing it between the wires in my mouth.

Those same spirits still pursued me, but their impressions were fading. I asked for a Bible, and the hospital's chaplain brought me one. He asked if I was a Christian, and I told him that Jesus had spoken to me when I was in hell.

He was kind, but I knew he didn't believe me. He wanted to know if I was a member of a church.

I said, "I haven't been to church in years."

He put the Bible on my nightstand. "You can call me if you need to talk."

"Thank you," I said. I knew he couldn't answer the questions I needed answering.

Again, the Bible became my best friend. I reread Ephesians, Galatians, Colossians, and Romans. At night, those same tormenting spirits continued to try to bring confusion.

They said, "Now you have to be good to go to heaven."

It was their same mantra, but something was emerging out of a depth within me. That tune of "You have to be good" was sounding like a fading voice more and more to me. I now realized that I had NOT been good, but Jesus Himself had spoken to me. I had been completely wrong in my attempt to make my life right. I wanted to "be good," and I wanted to go to heaven.

I read in Romans 10:9 that if you believe in your heart and confess with your mouth that Jesus is Lord, you will be saved. As I lay in my hospital bed, I thought I just wanted someone, anyone, to tell me they knew Jesus. I was very perplexed as to why only one young man wanted to confess that they knew Jesus.

After two weeks in the hospital, I was released. Coming home was challenging. What would be waiting for me?

I wasn't the same woman who went to the hospital over a two weeks ago. I wasn't sure who I was.

I wanted to see DeAnna, Ricky, and Scotty because I missed them. I even wanted to see Rick. I realized it wasn't him so much as it was a demon of murder operating through him. How could I accuse him when I had violated our marriage vows?

After walking, experiencing, and living this hell and going from an unseen spiritual realm back to the physical realm, I couldn't help but wonder: how I would respond in the days ahead? I wasn't sure if my experiences were beneficial or detrimental to my family and to me.

While driving into our apartment complex, my heart sped up. Even my anxiety over what might be waiting for me at home didn't keep me from becoming excited about finally seeing my kids and wrapping my arms around them.

I said to Rick, "I'm going to walk to my apartment on my own two feet. The last time I left here, you carried me. I will not be carried anymore. You're not carrying me this time. I'm walking."

"Sure, you can walk. It's your jaw that's wired, not your legs." He gave a light chuckle.

I realized that he didn't have a clue as to what I meant by that statement. The dark one had me carried out, but I was walking back to prove he had failed.

DeAnna, Ricky and Scotty approached me slowly, as if they were scared they would hurt me. I bent down and hugged them. They hugged me back. I knew they had lots of questions, but I was sure they had already heard talk. In their young minds, it was too hard for them to comprehend the scope of what had really happened.

I could see in their eyes that they were happy to have me back. "I missed ya'll so much," I mumbled through my wired jaw.

"Mama, you look like you have braces in your mouth," DeAnna said.

"How do you eat?" Ricky wanted to know.

Scotty just looked at me and snuggled close to me.

"I can sip through a straw but can't eat any more hamburgers." I tried to make this conversation light.

The routine in the Yarbrough house fell right back into place. I continued on as if all was normal. I was not a complainer, nor did I like attention. Those spirits were still around but had calmed down, making less of an impact on me now.

During my recovery, I had to take weekly trips back to the hospital. One of my doctors informed me that infection was trying to set in, and he was worried. He put me on some heavy liquid antibiotics. That didn't scare me because something inside me said, "You will not have an infection." This was a different voice, one with which I wasn't familiar.

After eight weeks, my wired jaw was set free. The kids and I enjoyed eating hamburgers together again. The first one I had in what seemed like a long time tasted really good.

Now being alone was much different than in previous weeks, when I kept hearing the repetitive mantra "You have to be good to get to heaven."

Not only was my jaw free, but I experienced freedom in so many ways, including being free for the bonds of religion. I knew being "good" didn't get you into heaven. The knowledge was a relief to my battle-worn mind. Still, I was unsure of some things as I tried to sort out the truth from the lies I had been told.

As I mentioned, things were slowly getting back to somewhat close to normal. Rick was working in construction, and the kids were in school. I now had the apartment to myself, and I cherished my time alone.

Since Rick was a musician, our apartment was different than most. Our apartment had gold shag carpeting, and a large black fishnet that cascaded from one wall to the next.

A makeshift bookshelf created out of two-by-fours and concrete blocks held Rick's vinyl record collections, which included some artists that most people hadn't heard of. Of course, the bookshelf also held stereo equipment consisting of a tuner, an amp, a record player, and a cassette deck.

Large stereo speakers stood in each corner of the living room. Psychedelic posters hung on the walls instead of pictures. I had inherited my grandmother's old upright piano that we put against the back wall.

One of my friends gave me a long, blue couch with cushions that consisted of different color designs. That was the only thing to sit down on except for a red, white and blue large bean bag chair that the kids loved to fall back on. Our television sat on a used old coffee table. Nothing was new, but I liked it.

Tattooed in the Palm of His Hand

While I was cleaning up the kids' cereal bowls starting my day I reflected back on what I had gone through never dreaming it would lead me to where I was now.

My thoughts were interrupted by the phone ringing.

"Hello?"

"Marsha, how are you?" It was my friend Cherry on the other end.

"Cherry, I'm good."

I had known Cherry since we were sixteen and went to school together. We both were eighteen when we had our first child. She married one of my childhood friends.

We spent some time catching up with each other. Then she told me about a church she had been attending and invited me.

"Marsha," she added, "the preacher's son has long hair too."

I knew she added that because of Rick's long hair.

I told her, "I've not been to church in a very long time, but I may see you there Sunday."

She gave me the time and address of the church, and we ended our conversation.

I thought, why not? I had already been to places that I never thought I would visit. I might as well add church to my repertoire of unusual places. After all, I was not completely unfamiliar with church although it had been years since I had gone to church.

I told Rick I had talked with Cherry and decided to go to church.

He said, "Okay, but I'm not going."

I mentioned it to the kids during a casual conversation, not making any promises in case I decided not to go. But when Sunday came, DeAnna, Ricky, Scotty, and I climbed in our car, and we drove to church.

I made a mental picture of what I thought this church should look like. I envisioned a small house church with a few people, mostly rural-type. I wasn't sure why I pictured it like that. I had never been to a house church and didn't know anyone who had.

As I pulled up, it was not anything I had imagined. It was a large brick church with a steeple and two separate adjacent buildings. I later learned held its Sunday school classes.

Cars filled its large parking lot and after driving around a few minutes I found a spot.

I couldn't help but wonder what kind of church it was. I opened the glass double doors and stepped into a medium-sized foyer. I stood there, all three of my children by my side.

Two teenage girls were hanging a poster on the bulletin board. Upon closer inspection, I noticed it was an advertisement for a car wash sponsored by the youth team. When they saw us, they both smiled, which made me feel welcome.

I had had mixed feelings about going to church. I had never been around "church people," and I wasn't sure if I wanted to be. Would they judge me, especially the way we were dressed? Those teenage girls wore dresses, but what would those in the church think of the way we were dressed?

I had never worn jeans to church, but I did on this day. My "Sunday best" consisted of bell-bottom hip-hugger jeans with butterfly patches, platform silver sparkly shoes, and a "hippie" shirt. I didn't even know if they would let me in with jeans. DeAnna and I looked like Cher, with our long waist-length, straight hair. The boys' blonde hair hung to their shoulders and wore bell-bottom jeans. My husband was in a rock-n-roll band, so my kids were used to the attire usually worn by musicians. Dressing this way was natural to us.

I peered through the glass doors that led into the sanctuary. Two rows of people were seated with a man standing in front of them. This had to be an adult or senior Sunday school class. It reminded me of my days as a shy child sitting with my grandpop in the adult Sabbath school class.

This church was larger than the one I attended as a child. The sanctuary contained long pews in the middle with shorter ones on each side. It had red carpet that matched the seats on the pews. Instead of stained glass windows, rectangular windows on each side wall let light inside the room.

A piano sat on one side of a large stage, along with some guitars on their stands and a set of drums. An organ sat on the other. Three stately chairs matching the color of the pews were positioned in the middle of the platform.

The choir loft directly behind the stage featured stadium-like seating, and their seats also matched the pews. The baptismal pool stood behind the choir with a large mural of John the Baptist baptizing Jesus hanging above it. I had never seen those in a church before.

Two men opened the sanctuary doors. Apparently, Sunday school had let out. The foyer filled with people of all ages.

I held Ricky's and Scotty's hands and stepped into the sanctuary. DeAnna walked close beside me. At that moment, I felt a love previously unknown to me. I received a big smile from a nice elderly lady. An inner peace settled in my spirit.

The pianist played an upbeat song. People talked with each other and found their seats in the pews.

I didn't know where to sit. I had to stop because I realized I had walked almost to the front of the church.

I quickly stepped into the third pew to my left. The kids slipped in next to me as I glanced around, hoping no one noticed me.

Only small kids and the youth sat in the front pews. One adult, a dark-haired lady, sat with them, and her seat was directly in front of us. Next to her was a boy she was trying to keep under control. He looked to be about the same age as DeAnna, maybe around ten. It looked as if she was there more from need than by choice.

The choir took their places in the seats behind the pulpit. All the musicians, including the guitar players and drummer, broke into song. I had never heard a band at church.

People in the congregation started clapping to the beat and singing a song. The words were projected on two large screens in front of the sanctuary. This was all so new to me.

Everyone stood, and some raised their hands. I took this in as I stood with the kids, observing it with curiosity.

I found myself in awe of the atmosphere in this place. Another upbeat song played, and the congregation continued to sing and clap. I could relate to them. I had been around enough musicians to know that people responded to music.

Like a trained band that knew how to transition to the next song without disturbing the mood, they moved into a slower song. The atmosphere changed to one of reverence, it felt like electricity was in the air.

Without anyone leading the congregation, the momentum slowed into a calm stillness. I watched as some of the people were lifting up their hands, as in surrender. I could sense they knew Jesus. I was so curious and intrigued by them.

Then the music stopped, like someone had unplugged every instrument. The pastor hadn't spoken one word. The choir slipped into silence, and like the congregation, most had hands raised and eyes shut.

The atmosphere again changed, this time to something mysterious, but it wasn't frightening. Rather, it was full of love and wonderment.

A blonde lady in the choir began to speak loudly in a different language. No one moved. I didn't understand any of this, but I knew this was of God. I was neither scared nor confused, but delighted, and I wanted to cry.

Then the dark-haired woman in front of me began to speak after the lady had stopped. She said, "The Lord has you tattooed in the palm of His hand, and He loves you."

Hot tears streamed down my face. I had found Him. My heart felt lighter, like the weight of guilt, shame, pain, deception, and distrust had lifted,

"I found Him, I found Him," was all I could say. "I found Him, the One who I had been searching for; the One who had spoken to me when I was so full of sin; the One who reached into the pit of hell and called me to Himself; the One who loved me in all of my shame; the One who fought for me when the evil one tried to kill me; the One who was inside of me without me inviting Him in.

I didn't understand any of this, but I didn't have to. I just knew that I had found Jesus.

Chapter Nine

THE PROPHECY

Freedom replaced the spirits of fear and doubt.

I had found Jesus, but I still had much to learn about Him. Life now had meaning and a purpose, but what exactly were they?

Rick started going to church. We didn't fit into the typical-looking young family at our church, but it didn't matter.

Rick, me, and the three kids had long hair and wore bell-bottom jeans. DeAnna's big brown eyes matched my own, whereas Ricky's and Scotty's blue eyes favored Rick.

Everywhere we went, people stared. Some were amazed at us while others were not so impressed. We had been called hippies. We weren't hippies at all although we looked the part. I would have labeled us a rock n roll family just as a country music family may dress in western attire.

Dale Zink was the pastor of Southside Assembly of God. He cared deeply about the souls of people getting saved. Everyone who wanted to attend church services was welcomed, regardless of their appearance. The church opened its doors to young people in jeans, flip-flops, tie-dye shirts, long hair, and hippies, most of who were teenagers.

Some called this move of God the Charismatic or the Jesus Movement, it was worldwide. The young people sat on the floor and in the aisles; they worshipped God with every inch of their being. A Jesus revolution had hit the world, and I was a part of it.

One Sunday evening, I asked a friend of mine to attend evening service with me. She hesitated at first, but she saw the change in me.

I couldn't stop talking about this Jesus. He had become everything to me. She told me that her father made her go to church when she was young. She related God to a big bully trying to control her every move, so she rebelled. I couldn't grasp her line of thinking. How could she perceive this beautiful, loving, kind God to be a dominating and controlling person?

She finally gave into my pleas to come and meet the Jesus I knew. When we arrived at church, it was packed. I had forgotten the church invited a guest speaker.

At first, I thought, *this isn't good.* I wanted her to hear my pastor.

We couldn't find any seats in the main sanctuary, so we made our way up to the balcony and settled there. DeAnna, Ricky, and Scotty were with us too because there wasn't a children's church that night. They wanted the children's workers to be in the service.

I'm sure that as kids, they all thought sitting in the balcony was way better than being downstairs. They had a bird's-eye view of everything.

The church seemed busier than usual this Sunday night. A lot of lightheartedness drifted through the air. People mingled in groups.

Men chatted with each other. Ladies smiled and laughed. Children giggled. I observed everything. Oh, how my heart and soul rejoiced! I was happy, content, and in love with all.

The band members and choir made their entrance, and the congregation found their seats. The pastor and guest speaker walked on the podium and sat in what I called the "holy-men chairs."

The guitarist hit his first note, and the other instruments joined in. The choir joined in with their voices in harmony, and I knew that heaven was pleased.

The congregation rose to their feet. No one had to ask them to stand. They just stood with their voices and hands lifted to the King of Kings.

I knew this was new to my friend, who stood next to me. I could identify with what she saw and felt. It had only been months earlier when I experienced comparable feelings and sights.

After several toe-tapping songs, the choir changed into a worship song. The electricity in the air was thicker than usual this night. The instruments stopped, and the choir broke into *Hallelujah*.

I wept as His presence engulfed the sanctuary. I wasn't ashamed of my tears, they were tears of thankfulness. How could I explain in words what my heart felt?

But I knew He knew, and I was satisfied. The choir sang a chorus of *Hallelujah*, acapella and then another voice was heard singing right after the choir stopped.

I thought someone in the congregation was singing. What a beautiful voice it was, clear and strong.

I watched as the choir members glanced at each other with baffled expressions, their eyebrows raised in confusion as they looked around the sanctuary. The people in the pews also looked around with similar perplexed expressions.

The lights in the church were brighter than I had ever seen them. A Presence had fallen in the church, and it was unexplainable.

My friend whispered, "Marsha, who is that singing?"

"I don't know," I whispered back.

The singing stopped. Some of the choir members softly wept. Even the men appeared humbled, kneeling down and placing their faces on the pews.

Both the men and the women responded in reverence. I could only weep with hands raised.

After a few minutes, the atmosphere changed. It was still wonderful, but not as thick.

The pastor rose and stood behind the podium. He said as a matter of fact, "Well, we just had one of the heavenly hosts come down and join us tonight."

I had heard an angel sing. This was too much for me, coming from such a dark world and then to enter this marvelous world full of light. It was more than I could have imagined.

How many people had the opportunity to hear a real angel sing?

The Gift

On a Wednesday night service, Rick was reunited with a long-time friend he hadn't seen in years, Samuel Sanders. Samuel had walked with the Lord longer than we had, and his excitement about Jesus was contagious. Samuel and Rick caught up with old memories, then Samuel asked Rick, "Have you received the baptism of the Holy Spirit?"

Rick asked, "What do you mean?"

I watched Samuel's eyes twinkled when Rick answered him. I knew Samuel wanted to continue this conversation. But I felt like it needed to be continued at our house.

"Samuel, would you like to come to our apartment tonight?" I spoke quickly and didn't look at Rick.

"Yeah, sure," Samuel replied.

"Great," I said and smiled.

I left hurriedly leaving both standing outside of the church while I went to pick up the kids from children's church. Rick was very selective as who came to our house, mostly his musician friends and a few others he trusted.

When Rick and I, moved in together, he didn't want any of my friends to come over to our apartment. He would say, "I can't trust them. They'll steal from me."

That should have been a red flag, but it went right by me. I told him he was crazy. I had known my friends since childhood. The children were also limited to having friends come over too.

No one would have ever thought Rick was an introvert. When Rick was on stage, writing music, in the studio, or jamming with a band, he came across as social. He was in his place, and he was very good too. He was confident in his God-given talent. At other times, though, his insecurities would rise, and he could be very difficult.

His birthday fell within the Gemini zodiac sign, and he bragged about being two people. I didn't believe in horoscopes, but in his case, it was probably true. He could change from moment to moment, which could be very frightening if you were on the receiving end.

But for now, I was happy I had expectancy and prayed silently as Rick drove home. We entered the apartment. The kids were excited to have a guest.

Ricky was asking Samuel questions as fast as a seven-year-old could. Scotty, always shy and stood nearby, taking it all in. He didn't participate, but he had complete confidence that his older brother would get the answers.

Of course, DeAnna was in tune with everything. She was much more mature than most ten-year-olds.

Samuel began the conversation, explaining who the Holy Spirit was that He was a Person. He showed us scriptures in the Bible verify everything. He was wise enough to introduce the Holy Spirit to us slowly and explained how He was God's Spirit left on earth to teach us all about Jesus. His explanations made me want this Wonderful Person even more.

I remembered the first time I heard the lady in the choir speak in a different tongue. Because of the atmosphere that accompanied it, I knew it was of God. I considered it to be a heavenly language.

I thought because they had this gift, they must be so close to God. I wished I could be one of them, but I doubted that could ever happen.

Samuel explained that speaking in an unknown tongue or language was a gift from God. The Lord wanted all His children to have it. Everything he said, he found scripture to support it, and I would read it.

Rick and the kids were listening too. I wanted this gift.

I had had enough of evil and darkness. I would do anything to keep them both in the past, never to have them raise their tormenting heads again.

Samuel asked, "Marsha, do you want to receive the Holy Spirit with the evidence of speaking in tongues? You received Him when you asked Jesus into your heart, but now you'll have His power, just like in the Book of Acts when Jesus told his disciples to wait until power came on them."

Oh, how I wished I would have had His power a few months back. I would have kicked butt. My mind kept going back to all the horror and pain I had experienced in my life.

"Yes, yes, and yes!" I said.

I wasn't ashamed about wanting this precious gift. I wasn't going to debate this issue either. This was a gift from my Heavenly Father.

Samuel said, "I'll lay hands on you. I'll then ask the Father to send the gift of speaking in tongues to you."

I stood up to accommodate Samuel and the Holy Spirit.

Samuel stopped and said, "There's something evil in this house. Do you have anything in here belonging to the occult, or have you opened the door and brought something in you aren't aware of?"

"No," I answered quickly.

He continued. "I'm sensing in my spirit that there is something the Holy Spirit wants out of here."

He started looking around the apartment. Then he stopped and asked the Holy Spirit to reveal it. He went straight over to our homemade-entertainment-system-plus-bookshelf unit. He picked up the book *Necromancy*, which is about communicating with the dead. It had belonged to my sister Donna Jean. She had moved and given me a box of books. She always read. Even as a child, she read many books. That was her hobby, so I figured it was just another one of her many, many books. She had a library of different books in different genres, from New Age to planting flowers.

Of course, I had never opened it. I just put it on my bookshelf along with several others to fill up space. I didn't pay any attention to the titles or topics.

Samuel immediately pulled it out, though. I was curious as to what kind of stuff was on its pages that would disturb the Holy Spirit. I truthfully didn't know what the word *Necromancy* meant.

I opened it up and thumbed through the pages. I understood why I needed this book out of our apartment. It contained actual photos of witch doctors that turned themselves into nonhuman-looking creatures. They were in other countries and openly practiced witchcraft.

I knew what I had experienced was nothing compared to what I saw in that book. I still wondered why those spirits taunted me. I had never dealt in the occult.

My mind went back to that mysterious man I had encountered when I worked at the airport, the one who said he had been sent to me. Was he the one who had opened up the door for me to experience the dark realm, and if so, why?

I pondered this in my heart but kept my thoughts to myself. I knew Satan wanted to destroy everyone that was his mission. What was sent to destroy me had lost, and the One who loved me beyond what I could perceive had rescued me.

Samuel asked if he could throw the book out, and suggested we burn it before tossing it into the dumpster, we all agreed.

The kids were absorbing all of this. I was glad they were getting a genuine lesson on the spirit world. It was real, a battle between evil and good.

So, we put the book in the kitchen sink and put a match to it. We watched as the pages crinkled under the small flame that crept upon and consumed those pages.

As the book burned, we all sang songs of praises and rejoiced before the Lord. We marched out of the apartment like soldiers, following behind Samuel who held the ashes of the burnt book. He dropped the burnt book in the dumpster and slammed the lid down.

We knew we had won this battle. How dare the evil ones try to stop the Holy Spirit from giving us His gift? I thought, *how stupid is the devil? He'll never be able to stop anyone from receiving this free gift from God.*

After we destroyed the evil source in those pages, we returned to the apartment.

Samuel said, "Let's continue with the Lord's work."

He began to pray, telling the Lord how good, merciful, and kind He is. Our living room began to fill with His Presence.

Samuel again explained that the Holy Spirit wanted each of His children to have the gift of speaking in tongues from the Father. The Holy Spirit was free, and only by grace alone was He obtained.

I wanted so much more of Him. Samuel laid his hands on my head and prayed again for the infilling of the Holy Spirit.

Samuel asked me to open my mouth and just move my tongue, that the Holy Spirit would fill me with His language. I would then speak directly to God, and it would be a perfect prayer.

He showed me 1 Corinthians 14:2 in the Bible. I read aloud, "For anyone who speaks in a tongue does not speak to people but to God. Indeed, no one understands them they utter mysteries by the Spirit."

I heard a mumbling sound come from deep within me. My tongue moved, and I gave voice to it. I knew I now had this wonderful gift.

I was elated and felt as if I had stepped into another world. This time it was a clean, pure world.

I couldn't explain anything and I didn't want to try. Only the Lord knew what the Holy Spirit spoke through me. This experience was too much, it was wonderful.

Words couldn't articulate what I felt. Jesus had taken all my pain, shame and guilt away and He had given me a gift that I didn't deserve.

God Speaks

Joy filled my days now. The uncertainty of whether I could be good enough to go to heaven had left. I knew beyond anything that I wanted to please Him.

Rick also received the wonderful gift of speaking in tongues several days later. The Yarbrough's were finally on the right road.

Rick wanted to put together a Jesus band and I agreed. I knew music was who he was.

Jesus had captured me, and I wanted to capture others.

Weeks turned to months, and we were happy. I felt like we were like *The Brady Bunch*.

Rick became more anxious about playing music. We prayed and sought the Lord for Christian musicians and what direction to take. We were what Christian's called 'babies in the Lord'.

One Wednesday night while getting ready to go to service, Rick seemed more agitated and discouraged. I knew his patience was wearing thin, his prayer wasn't being answered as quickly as he wanted.

Before we left the apartment, he spoke out loud, "Lord, I need an answer, and I need it tonight. Let the youth pastor or the pastor give me the answer."

I knew he meant it, and I agreed with a big *amen*. We went to church and afterwards, several of the members talked with us, but no one said anything about music to Rick.

We returned to the apartment. When we walked in, Rick shut and locked the door. I knew he was upset.

"F***, Jesus!" I had heard that voice before come out of Rick. I never wanted to hear it again.

Fear gripped me. The living room turned black, and those evil shadows appeared again.

I sat down on the couch and watched as he walked down the hall towards our bedroom. Evil had invaded my world again. How could that be? Where was Jesus?

A force greater than me literally pulled me up to my feet. I felt it guide me down the hall toward the bedroom. I was scared. Memories flooded my mind like a tidal wave. No, no, this could not be happening again!

I entered the bedroom. Rick lay across the bed with an old acoustic guitar in his hands. He had tears in his eyes.

He didn't look like the maniac who scared me. He reminded me of a hurt little boy who had been promised something he didn't get.

The air in the room seemed fresher than the other parts of the house. I stood in front of my husband.

Then someone begin to speak through me. "Keep your eyes off the church. Keep your eyes off of man. My children won't come to Me. I will go to them. It will be bigger and better and nationwide."

The bedroom filled with what seemed to be a foggy, smoke-like dewy substance. It didn't stay long, but it felt like I was seeing the world through foggy glasses.

Rick said, "That wasn't you. That had to be the Holy Spirit speaking through you."

I had never experienced anything like that. I fell to my knees and gave praises to the Lord. Rick had gotten a word from the Lord, although it came from an unexpected messenger.

We continued to go to church and prayed as a family. I had the family I had always wanted. Except for the dog, the apartment complex did not allow dogs. But oh! Well I had Jesus and the Holy Spirit was becoming my best friend.

Chapter Ten

AN ANGEL AND STITCHES

I was truly happy. Joy overflow in my life. But of course, life is not like a movie where you can rewrite the ending if it doesn't please you. One thing I did know was that life is forever changing, and change is ever present.

I can't give a timeline when everything seemed to change. I'm not sure when change crept in unnoticed or when it announced itself and took center stage. Regardless of how change arrived, its arrival was not a source of comfort.

Rick became discouraged trying to put a Jesus band together. His discouragements carried into old battles that caused chaos in what was our happy home.

Rick had quit his construction job, and money became an issue. I sensed changes were on the horizon from previous experiences, and I knew that this change would not be a good one. Peace floated out the door. If only the kids and I could have departed with it. I had tasted peace and prayed desperately for it to return.

Friday nights were usually spent watching *Sanford and Son*. I tried to make it a fun night. If we had the money I would have pizza delivered. This Friday evening, money was short so the kids and I drove to the grocery store to buy frozen pizza, with some cookies for dessert.

We had just bought a 1967 Chevrolet Malibu from Rick's sister Shirley and her husband. We were still making payments on it.

We were on our way home from the store. DeAnna sat in the passenger's seat, and Ricky and Scotty stood on the floorboard in the backseat. Still no law for seatbelts.

I turned from the four-lane street onto a two-lane road, one block away from our apartment complex. Suddenly, everything went black. I could feel the car swirling and spinning, and it seemed like the spinning would never end. I wasn't sure what had happened. My mind had not yet comprehended that we had been in a car wreck.

Everything seemed to stand still. The impact of the collision had knocked me unconscious for a few seconds. After coming to my senses, I immediately turned my head toward the backseat. What I saw were two sets of blue wide-opened eyes on the face of blonde-headed little boys; scared and confused, just like me. I looked at DeAnna and saw her pants were torn and that a large piece of skin protruded from her jeans. She was calm and not crying, though. The door of the glove box had been thrown open, and I knew her leg had hit it.

I was amazed at how calm I was too. My kids were my life.

In a matter of minutes, people had surrounded our car. I could hear them asking if we were okay.

A lady handed DeAnna a towel through the passenger's side window. I looked down, and her pants were now soaked in blood.

The door to the passenger's side flew open, and a young man knelt down at eye level with DeAnna. He said, "I'm a volunteer fireman. I've called rescue from my radio."

I asked him, "Are you a Christian?"

He replied, "Yes."

I said, "Let's all grab hands and pray."

Ricky, Scotty, DeAnna, the fireman, and I all held hands while I prayed. As I prayed I kept my eyes open. I saw an evil darkness had invaded the car and it was darker on the inside than the outside but above our heads a circle of a bright light surrounded all four of us. I found it odd that it didn't settle on the fireman, who was still kneeling by DeAnna. I didn't know why that light didn't include him.

After our prayer, I realized we had been in a car wreck. We were in a church parking lot on the corner of our street. I was about to turn onto this road when we got hit. My car had been thrown off the two-lane road.

Cars were stopping, and people were coming from everywhere wanting to help. The police were directing traffic.

I heard someone say we were hit head-on by a large Mercury sedan driving on the wrong side of the road.

The lady who had handed DeAnna the towel lived in the parsonage on the church grounds. I am sure she prayed for us.

I heard the rescue sirens coming. Two ambulances arrived, and the medics evaluated all of us. DeAnna was lifted onto the stretcher. The boys were carried off in the arms of two of the medics, and I was helped to the ambulance. They let all of us ride together. The boys sat next to me and DeAnna was on the stretcher. I had all my kids with me. They were breathing, and I couldn't see any serious injuries except for the one on DeAnna's leg. However, she handled all of this like a trooper. I was thankful.

They took us to the same hospital I had stayed in when my jaw had been broken. When we arrived at the ER, they separated us. This scared me. I didn't want to leave my children.

The doctors gave orders to the nurses that each of us had to be x-rayed. I was amazed at how calm my children were. Of course, after the nurses saw I was stable, I went from bed to bed checking on all of my kids.

I knew DeAnna had the worst injuries. The boys were banged up and bruised, but otherwise all right. I was proud of them, they were tough little guys.

DeAnna received more attention from the staff, so her room stayed filled with medical personnel. The boys enjoyed the popsicles the nurses brought them while we waited for the results of our X-rays. When the results came back, the doctor gave me strict orders not to walk anymore. I had a broken bone in my knee. It was throbbing, but I never thought it was broken. He said, "We've called in a specialist for DeAnna. She has a broken nose and a severe gash in her leg. Which will require more than just surface stitches, she needs immediate microscopic surgery.

I wanted to be with DeAnna. I asked for a wheelchair, and the nurse accommodated me. Once the doctors determined that the boys' X-rays showed no broken bones or internal injuries, Ricky was moved into the same bed as Scotty.

Rick arrived at the hospital an hour later. He said he had been wondering why we hadn't returned home from the store. When he drove to the corner searching for us, he saw the blinking red lights from the fire trucks and police cruisers. The police were still on the scene rerouting traffic. Several people were still gathered at the crash site. Rick than began to give me a moment by moment detailed description of what he had gone through.

. He said "I felt like time froze for a moment. I saw my red Chevrolet, its motor completely smashed-in. The wreck knocked the motor off its mounts, and the grill was shoved up and under the hood. And the left front tire was flat. "

"The policeman was waving at me to go, but I couldn't move. I told him that I wasn't going and pointed at my car. I yelled, "That's my car over there!"

"The cop stopped traffic and came over to me. He asked me my name and the name of my wife. He went back to his car, I guess to make sure I was telling the truth. Then he told me ya'll had been transported to the hospital.

"I couldn't remember driving to the hospital. After seeing the condition of the car, I didn't know what I'd find.

"When the triage nurse found out I was the husband and father of the family in the wreck, they allowed me to come back to see you. I'm so glad everyone's in one piece." He kissed and hugged me and each of the kids.

The ER doctor told us he was waiting for the specialist to come.

I knew it would be a while before he came. I was told they were keeping DeAnna in the hospital to operate on her broken nose the next morning.

Rick suggested I call my mother. She was playing bingo at a Catholic church on the same side of town. One of the nurses heard us mention the name of the church.

She said, "I go there. I know who to call to get a message to your mother."

She was God-send. She called directly into the church's after-hours number.

About an hour later, my mother walked in with fear written all over her face. After hugging and kissing all of us, she calmed down.

My mother suggested taking the boys to her house for the night.

Rick told her, "We'll be coming over after we get DeAnna settled in from her knee surgery."

I kissed the boys goodbye and watched as they were rolled out in wheelchairs to my mother's car.

One Hundred and Fifty Stitches

My adrenaline was slowing down and I asked if I could get a shot for pain. Like many mothers, you're the last one standing you're not concerned about nothing but your children. She smiled and replied "I was just waiting on you to ask."

I sat in the wheelchair next to DeAnna's bedside. She hadn't cried and was acting so grown up, chatting with the doctors and nurses as they came and went.

The doctor finally arrived. He was friendly enough after introducing himself to us but was focused on DeAnna. He playfully flirted with her a little, talking about her big, beautiful brown eyes, doing his best to put her at ease.

They had already given her several shots to numb the area around that deep gash on her leg and had started an IV. Now they were getting down to the problem.

We watched as the nurse draped a green surgical cloth over DeAnna's leg. This was the first time I had really seen her injury. I had been hobbling from child to child. I understood why the attending ER physician decided to call in a specialist it was deep and her tissues and ligaments were exposed.

He made small talk with DeAnna and asked her several questions as he administered several more numbing shots to her leg. She answered his questions. I was sure the IV had some medication in it to keep her calm without putting her under anesthetic. They asked me kindly if I would leave, I told them that I would not be in the way but I would stay right outside so DeAnna could see me.

The doctor slowly and methodically sewed inside the deep gash. After over one hundred fifty stitches, her ordeal was finished. Ten-year-old DeAnna had endured it with courage.

The doctor complimented her and said, "I'll see you tomorrow."

The nurse told us DeAnna's room was ready and that she would be taken there now. She told me to kiss her goodbye since I hadn't been discharged from the emergency room yet, I wasn't allowed to go with her. I kissed her, and Rick accompanied her to her room.

Tears filled my eyes for the first time. It had been several hours since the wreck. I was relieved to know that this was coming to an end and it wasn't as bad as it could have been.

One of the nurses wheeled me back to my original ER bed. The doctor told me, "Okay, Mama. Now it's your turn. All of your kids are taken care of."

He showed me the X-ray of my knee. He pointed out the small bone called the patella, also known as the kneecap. It had a hairline fracture. My knee must have hit the steering wheel.

The doctor told me it would heal without surgery. He then wrapped it in a brown Ace bandage and asked the nurse to bring me crutches.

She returned with some aluminum crutches and asked me to stand up. I complied, rising from the wheelchair. She then told me to put the crutches under my arms, to make sure they were the right size for my height and arm length.

I had never used crutches, and it felt awkward. She gave me a quick lesson in maneuvering them.

Then she stated, "Don't put any weight on your right leg. She handed me my discharge papers with instructions to be follow up by an orthopedic doctor in three days.

"Where are the elevators? And will you give me my daughter's room number?"

"Visiting hours ended long ago. Your daughter's in good hands. You should probably just wait for your husband."

I knew she was right, but still I wanted to see DeAnna. About that time, Rick stepped into the ER waiting room.

I waved him over. "Rick, will you take me to see DeAnna?"

His eyes dropped from exhaustion. "She's already asleep. They gave her a pain pill after her surgery. She's not even going to know you're there."

"Okay," I said reluctantly. Exhaustion and fatigue had claimed me.

I would see her tomorrow. DeAnna's surgery for her nose was in the afternoon, which was a plus for me. I knew I needed rest, and this gave me a little extra time.

The next day, I was able to hobble behind her as they wheeled her in for surgery. She stayed another night at the hospital. We stayed at my mother's house for the weekend and then returned to our apartment.

Afterwards, DeAnna and I had to make trips back and forth to the doctors. Her leg took several months to heal. She was so strong and determined. She went back to school after three weeks of being homebound. She handled it with such courage.

We all talked about the accident a couple of weeks afterwards. I retold the story of all of us praying. I had not mentioned to anyone the circle of light I had seen around our heads when we prayed, or about the darkness inside the car.

Ricky spoke up. "Mama, did you see that angel tie that gold bow around our heads?"

I was thrilled and astonished that Ricky had seen it and described what I had seen in such a beautiful way. That an angel had tied a gold bow around our heads.

Not only did my son confirm it, but the Lord had let him see the angel. Once again, the angel of the Lord had penetrated the darkness.

Hundred-Dollar Bill

Rick's inability to put a Christian band together caused him to grow impatient and with that brought anger.

He was not only a musician but a songwriter. His talent burned inside of him, but now was being stagnated. Since he wasn't playing music, his attitude had become unbearable.

Musicians and artists can be very temperamental people. Rick had acquired a reputation of being unpredictable and difficult to work with despite being a great musician.

I began to see the old Rick slowly creeping back in. I continued to pray, but the handwriting was on the wall, so to speak. The happiness and stability I had were gradually crumbling away.

Again, no money was coming into the household. Rick refused to work. Instead, he spent his time searching for musicians to put another band together with the promise of bringing money in through music. We were sinking financially. For us to survive, I had to make money quick.

I reapplied to Jax Liquors, a company I worked with in the past. I was hired immediately as a bartender, which was a relief to me. They assigned me to work at The Spectrum, a well-known newly opened lounge.

The Spectrum had earned a reputation of being one of Jacksonville's favorite places to go. This was when disco was just becoming a craze.

I never dreamed they would want me to bartend there. The Spectrum's bartenders were known to be beautiful. We were required to wear sexy uniforms and go-go boots. I considered myself average-looking. I was slender with straight, long, dark hair and brown eyes. I certainly was not Playboy material.

One night, at the beginning of my shift, the bartenders began telling me about the nice-looking gentlemen sitting at our horseshoe-shaped bar.

"Marsha," one of the bartenders said, "That's your station. We've been serving him until your shift. He has a hundred-dollar bill sitting next to his drink, but he's buying five-dollar drinks and leaving the change."

"Really?" I thought that was strange, but I understood why she told me this. The lounge rule was all tips had to be placed in the tip jar, and we split the tips at the end of the night. All of us made good money.

One of the bartenders was still talking with the man. I watched them for a few minutes before setting up my station.

I waited for Linda, to end her conversation. She was not only talking but flirting with the man. She was attractive with platinum-blonde hair, a full figure, and blue eyes with false eyelashes.

I approached him and introduced myself. "Hi, my name's Marsha. I'll be your bartender now, but you want to keep Linda as your bartender, that's okay too."

I wanted to let him know that regardless of him being my customer, I had no problem with him keeping Linda. She worked for an attorney during the week and a bartender for extra money on the weekends.

Linda had been serving him, and he seemed to enjoy her company. She was a nice person, recently divorced. I knew she needed some man to validate her, and I felt a little sad for her. I had worked with women who were always looking for men.

He said, "No, that's okay. You're my bartender. You're cute. Linda's sexy, but you're cute."

I thanked him and smiled. Linda and the other bartender knew I was okay with them continuing to serve him. They both continued to flirt with him. I saw his hundred-dollar bill, but it seemed to entice them more than it did me.

The bar got busy, and all the bartenders had to return to their stations. I checked on this man to ask if he wanted another drink. He was handsome with dark hair and light-colored eyes. He wore a nice, dark, expensive-looking suit, and possessed a lot of self-confidence.

"Marsha," he remembered my name. "You're really cute. You remind me of a free, hippie-type of chick."

A hippie-type chick? Plus, he threw in the word free. I knew what he was thinking.

He continued. "I date women like Linda all the time, I have never dated anyone like you."

"Really," I replied, already knowing where this conversation was going.

This was not the first time this had happened. I had been a bartender for several years and heard all of the pick-up lines from men. I waited to hear if he could come up with an original line to continue this discussion.

He surprised me with his directness. "I would like to take you out to breakfast tonight after you close. I can come back and get you. I'm staying at a hotel downtown."

I would have really liked to have had more of a conversation with him before he became so straightforward. I wasn't a shallow woman who wanted or needed a man to feed me lines. I preferred discussing issues with men and getting their perspectives on certain topics.

"Well, you really want to take me to breakfast, right?" I asked with a half-smile.

I thought, *this man doesn't read people well. I hadn't given him one clue that I was interested in him.*

"Yes, I would love to take you to breakfast," he answered like he had just scored with me. I knew it wasn't me, though. It was the chase.

His fingers touched the hundred-dollar bill still lying beside his glass of Scotch. He hadn't touched that money anytime during his conversation with Linda or with me. His eyes met mine.

I thought, does he really think his money and looks impress me? How shallow of a woman does he think this little dark-haired hippie chick is?

I walked away without answering him. Linda and the other bartender wanted to know what he asked me, so I told them.

Linda smiled. "Marsha, just tell him yes, that you'll go to breakfast. That can't hurt anything. If you do, he'll leave you that one-hundred-dollar-bill. We know you're not going to breakfast, but he doesn't know that."

I walked back to where he sat. I said, "I've thought about the breakfast invitation. It sounds good to me, except there is just one small request I need to make."

"Anything," he smiled.

"Before we go, you'll have to take me to my house to pick up my husband and three kids. I know they'll enjoy meeting you and having breakfast with you as well. I'll only go if my family is invited. Otherwise, no thank you."

He just smiled at me, picked up his hundred-dollar bill, and left. When he walked out of the lounge, I knew Linda and the others would be upset with me for not playing the game.

They asked what I said to him, and I told them. All they could say was, "Marsha!" and sigh like kids do when they don't get their own way.

Regardless, I felt good. When you do what is right, it will always come back to you in one way or another. I knew I had won, not his money but his respect, which was something money couldn't buy.

Two weeks had gone by since the incident with the hundred-dollar man. Then on a Saturday night after the bar closed, the bartenders and waitresses were cleaning up. The manager received a phone call.

He said loud enough for all of us to hear, "Mr. Romano, Jax Liquors District Manager, is in town and on his way over to talk with us."

We all gave each other that *wonder-what-he-wants* look. This was very unusual, since Mr. Romano never made a visit at closing time. This news could be good, or it could be bad.

On the weekends, we hired extra help because we were so busy, and it took longer to clean up. By the end of the night, everyone wanted to go home. The bartenders, waitresses, and our manager waited impatiently at the bar.

Finally, Mr. Romano walked in with two guys as well as the gentleman who had asked me to breakfast. Right away, Linda shot me a confused look, which I returned.

My heart sped up a little. My mind raced as I tried to recall if I had said or done anything that would get me reprimanded. I felt weird seeing my district manager with that man.

Mr. Romano walked behind the bar so he could address the entire staff.

"First off, I must inform you that you have been under strict surveillance here. We work to maintain the highest form of honesty and integrity in this company. We strive to have a reputation of respect." His Italian style was right out of the *Godfather* movie. He had a reputation of being a man who ran his father in-law's business with a professional and firm hand. He was handsome with coal-black hair and dark brown eyes, and always dressed in a dark suit and nice shoes. His demeanor demanded respect without speaking.

I could feel everyone stiffen up. We all glanced at our manager. He looked concerned, and his forehead wrinkled a bit while his blue eyes glanced at his bartenders and waitresses.

"This gentleman right here," Mr. Romano said, indicating the gentleman who had asked me to breakfast. "He is who we call our integrity and honesty detective. He goes to all our lounges and spies on our employees. Then he reports back to me."

Now my hands were sweating. The voice in my head was saying, *you're in big trouble now. You were being too rude.*

"He always carries one-hundred-dollar bills to each lounge," he continued. "This is to lure anyone who would rather have money than protect the integrity of our company.

"Marsha," he said, looking straight at me. I felt like he was about to sentence me. "You've proven yourself to be a woman of integrity and honesty. You were courteous and represented this company well. This is your one-hundred-dollar bill that you don't have to share with anyone."

With that, he clapped and handed me the one-hundred-dollar bill. I thanked him, and the gentleman who had asked me to breakfast came and gave me a hug. Money wasn't what made that night, it was respect. You can't buy respect.

This is the grace that Jesus gives, and I had experienced that wonderful grace. You can't respect others if you don't respect yourself.

Jesus had given me respect even after all the inner turmoil and hurt. This event made me know and realize that nothing could make me see myself as anything else but a woman of honor.

Respect comes from within. A person may go through life with guilt, and they may lose respect for themselves. Yet, when you ask Jesus into your life, He doesn't remember your past so all of your guilt and shame is gone.

If Jesus sees your heart and forgives you, then why is it so hard for others or yourself to forgive?

Chapter Eleven

GRANDMA'S HOUSE

Paying the bills became much more difficult as time went on. In fact, we couldn't pay them. It was pointless trying to reason with Rick to get a job besides just playing music on the weekends. I had been down that road too many times and it caused nothing but arguments.

At that point, we had two options. We could either be homeless or move to my grandmother's house. The choice to move to my grandma's house was not one that I wanted to choose, but it was better than being homeless.

My grandmother had died earlier that year, leaving her house vacant. Since her house was located in an older, declining neighborhood, leaving it unoccupied was asking for trouble. Unfortunately, the neighborhood had attracted drug pushers and everything else that thrives in that environment.

A transient had broken into her house and started a small fire. The elderly neighbor who lived next door saw a flicker of light coming through one of the bedroom windows. She immediately called the police. When they arrived, they arrested the transient for vagrancy. Thank God, the fire caused very little damage

Before making this decision, I spoke at length with my mother, because she had inherited Grandma's house. We both agreed our moving in was the only solution.

Initially, I was concerned about the children living in such a neighborhood, but as it turned out, another family with kids lived on the same street. They became great friends. In fact, everyone in the neighborhood was just trying to survive, so we fit in just fine.

After we moved, I quit my job as a bartender. Working long hours and arriving home at three in the morning was taking a toll on me. I still had all the responsibilities of being a wife and mother, plus the burden of paying the bills.

My daily life was chaotic, and with very little money, life was hard. If something broke, which often happened in an old house, we either had to wait until I could make arrangements for someone to fix it, or we simply did without it. When the old refrigerator went out, my only solution was to buy a Styrofoam cooler and fill it with ice daily for several weeks.

I begged Rick, "We need money. The lights will be turned off today."

He stomped into the bedroom and shut the door. I cringed inside. Why didn't he want to take care of his family? Those types of reactions from him left me feeling desperate.

I silently cried out to God, asking, "Why, God, why?"

I found myself blaming God. I asked, "Why aren't you doing something?"

I was losing my faith. The Holy Spirit allowed me to vent and continue with my self-centeredness and blaming Him. All along, I knew inside that He was the One who kept me. I should have been thankful. Of course, God's love never changes according to our actions, even when we are being ridiculously stupid.

I still held onto the promise the Lord gave me. "My children won't come to me. I will go to them. It will be bigger and better and nationwide. Keep your eyes off the church; keep your eyes off of man."

I had no doubt that it was Jesus who spoke that. I didn't understand why we were having such difficulties. I prayed and sought the Lord without any answers.

"You've Been to Hell?"

My mother worked for the school board, so I asked mom, if she could help me get a job there.

She knew I needed a job and told me she would see what she could do. She had worked with them for over thirty years and was well respected and liked.

I was relieved when she told me they had positions opened. First, I had to take a typing test. I was surprised I had passed it, as I had not used my typing skills for years.

The school board hired me as a clerk typist. I went to work immediately. I was assigned to the media arts department.

After being at my job for several weeks meeting my co-workers we begin to get to know each other. I certainly lived a different lifestyle than most of my them. I was married to a long-haired musician who didn't work. I hung out with rock musicians and their wives or girlfriends, and we smoked pot.

My work wardrobe was different than the other girls in my office as well. I dressed in bell bottoms while most of the others wore office attire. They wore nice pumps, whereas my shoes were two-inch wedges with silver glitter.

Most of them visited their beauticians weekly while I kept my dark hair long and straight.

We all ate lunch together and enjoyed sharing some of our personal stories. After getting beyond my outward appearance, I fit right in. We talked mostly about family and our weekend experiences. It was ladies getting together being able to talk freely with each other. We shared laughs and our troubles too. One confided in me privately that her husband was having an affair. I felt sorry for her and all I could tell her was I would pray for her.

They always wanted me to share, especially if Rick and the band had a music gig. After the band ended the night we would end up at a twenty-four-hour restaurant, usually at Denny's restaurant. The guys would talk about music and the wives we've talk about whatever. These were the times when Rick was the happiest. He felt complete.

Then Rick and I would go home, smoked a joint, and sit out on the front porch swing. Sometimes we talked until dawn. He would get his old acoustic guitar and strummed it while talking to me. He played some of the new songs he was writing and explained what key they were be played in. He often added a little harmonica, or "blues harp" as he called it, to a song.

These were good times for both of us. He could take me to a different world, and I easily got caught up in his creativity. His blue-green eyes lit up when those riffs came together.

At times, I reflected back on my first encounter with this musician, realizing he hadn't changed. He was still one with his music. It was me who had changed.

The girls at work were surprised when they found out who my mother was. She was well respected on her job, she had been in the same department over twenty – five years, and in fact it was just her and her supervisor for years. She was a very attractive and classy lady with dark brown eyes. She parted her black-and-gray short hair down the middle, and two beautiful, silvery gray natural waves framed her face. Those waves looked as if she spent time to get them just right. She was frequently asked if her hair was naturally that color or if she had frosted it. My mother's slender frame could wear anything, and everything looked nice on her. She always dressed nicely, even around the house. She was one of the first bookkeepers to be hired by the Duval County School Board. She only possessed a ninth-grade education, but she had a natural connection with numbers. She later took a bookkeeping class when she turned eighteen.

I wanted everyone to know about Jesus. He was so real to me. It's like having the best gift in the world and knowing it had to be shared. I wanted to share my experience of hell to warn people that hell is real. Even though several years had passed since that experience, it was still fresh in my memory.

I was assigned to work on a project that required me to interact closely with an administrator from another department. She was an older woman with dyed auburn hair. Her husband was a retired principal of one the oldest high schools in Jacksonville. They had met in college, and both wanted to be teachers. They had accomplished their goal. She left teaching to work as an administrator with the school board. She continued working on her doctorate in education. I liked her, but we were as different as two women could have been.

During the two weeks we worked together, we became friends. She told me that her and husband had decided not to have kids of their own. They considered their students to be their own children, so according to her, she had hundreds of kids. I wasn't sure if she thought she made the right decision or not. Regardless, I respected that they kept that commitment with each other.

We had only days left to finish our project, which, as she put it, was "coming together splendidly." She gave me several compliments concerning our team effort. I knew she viewed me as a student, which was ok with me.

We had one more day left before our project was completed. I felt in my heart that I needed to tell her what I had experienced concerning my trip to hell.

I hadn't told her much about myself. I hesitated doing so because she was very analytical. She didn't intimidate me, but her academic accomplishments made me wonder if I should share my experience. I wasn't sure what her reaction would be.

As I drove to work, I knew it would be my last day with my friend. The question whirling around my head was how to share my experience with her. I wanted her to meet this wonderful man named Jesus, the One with whom I had fallen in love with.

I knew her life was void. She lacked Him in her life. Despite her achievements, which was self-performance driven this left her soul empty. She was never completely satisfied. I knew no matter how many degrees or accomplishments one earns, it never really satisfies them.

I prayed in my spirit most of the way to work. I asked the Holy Spirit to lead me in this attempt to make Jesus known to her.

She greeted me with her usual, "Good morning Marsha," as I walked into the office.

I put my purse under my desk. "Yes, it is a good God-morning." I had never put God in our good-morning greetings.

She stood by the window watering a small plant. I watched her eyes wondering if she caught that word. She proceeded to her desk and opened her briefcase. This was her routine.

I sat down at my desk, which faced hers. She looked rested, so I knew she must have had a good night's sleep. I also noticed she had colored her hair a deeper shade of auburn.

"Well, we have finished." she said with a smile. "I want to thank you for your help on this project. You have typed and retyped this language art curriculum. Today we just need to proofread the last portion of it."

I said, "I have really enjoyed working with you."

"Thank you, Marsha. I have to admit, when you first came to me, I wasn't sure if I could work with you. When they told me your mother was Mrs. Young, I was taken back." She laughed.

"I know. I've heard that before. You can't judge a book by its cover, as the saying goes."

This was an opportunity for me to tell her about the One who had changed my life from the inside. Those secrets that dwell within the heart of a person are kept in those dark places where failures, fears, doubts, bitterness, rejections and jealousy grow. I had experienced all those feelings and had tried to hide them, even from myself. But the more the Holy Spirit introduced Jesus to me, I was confident that I could trust Him to conquer all the lies the enemy had told me. I was free from me.

My personality didn't change any but now all guilt and confusion had gone. I had a self-confidence that wasn't based on my own doings. I knew I was loved for who I was. I was still bound by some habits which most self-righteous or religious people would have condemned me to hell, but my soul was free and I wanted her to be free too.

I asked, "Do you believe in God?"

She thought for a moment before replying in her authoritative voice, "Well, I believe that there may be a higher power, but I do not believe in a personal god. I think there could be many gods, or whatever titles, labels or names people use is ok with me. But man has invented many gods, throughout the beginning of the world. So many different religions, I believe whatever you feel comfortable with is fine. But me personally, I believe more in the scientific theory of evolution or a super intelligence way beyond the human intellect."

During her explanation of explaining her belief she kept her dignified voice. It was the same tone she used when speaking with her superiors about changing the project on which we had been working.

I had never encountered an educational person when telling my story, but I had shared it numerous times with our musician friends and others. They accepted this without question and were like, "Wow, what a trip." They believed in Jesus, and they knew they were in need of a Savior.

I felt intimation rising up within me. My heart beat faster, and my mind kept telling me, "You're out of your league. Stop before you make a fool of yourself."

However, I could not be intimidated by this spirit. At the cost of appearing ridiculous, I continued.

"You're right. There is a higher being that is far more intelligent than us. I know Him." I left it at that, hoping she would ask me who.

Her eyes smiled while she asked me that wonderful question. "Who may I ask is this?" Her voice contained a hint of sarcasm.

"His name is Jesus."

"Oh, you're a Jesus believer, a Christian. That's nice, Marsha." Now she patronized me.

"Yeah, but I didn't meet Him in church. I met Him in hell."

"So, you believe in hell too?" she quickly shot back.

"Not only do I believe in it, but I've been there," I retorted.

"You've been to hell?" She quickly asked with a smirk.

"Yep, that's where I met Jesus. He is the only One who can stop you from going to hell."

"Tell me about this, Marsha. I don't believe I have ever met someone who has gone to hell. I've heard some say, 'Why don't you go to hell?' I'm sure no one has reported back from hell." A mocking spirit had now manifested.

"There is a hell, and demons live there. It's a place that not even the worst of the worst should go. The torment and darkness are beyond description. Satan himself dwells there." I felt the Holy Spirit taking over. The battle had begun. I understood what was happening in the spirit realm. Darkness wanted her to stay ignorant. I liked her, and I wanted her to know that Jesus loved her.

"Truly, I have experienced it. If you don't believe me, ask my mother. She was there. I literally had demons bite me on my back." I said.

Her eyes widened as I continued. I watched her take all our hard work in manila folders out of her briefcase. She proceeded to put them on top of her desk in neat stacks. I had watched her do this every morning over the last two weeks.

I wondered if this conversation was over. How could she just leave a statement like that and not question it?

She folded her hands in front of her. Her classroom-teacher mannerism was in place to do battle with this uneducated, misguided pupil, namely me. I knew she was used to taking command, but what she was not prepared for was what I was about to communicate.

My experience wasn't out of a book. I felt like the Prophet John when he wrote his epistle 1 John 1:1: "We proclaim to you the one who existed from the beginning, whom we have heard and seen. We saw him with our own eyes and touched him with our own hands. He is the Word of life."

I had an experience, and she had no frame of reference for it. No, I had not touched nor saw him but I had heard his voice.

"Okay, Marsha," she said. "Explain to me what you mean. You have gone to hell. Please give me the details of the demons that actually bit your back."

"I know it sounds ridiculous," I stated. "Several years ago, I went on an adventure that I wasn't prepared for. I was in a bad marriage and wanted out.

"I worked as a bartender and befriended another bartender. She turned out to be a witch. I decided to move to Miami to start afresh and she wanted to go too. She was from the west coast, we were completely opposite personalities.

"A busboy from the lounge also joined us on this trip. I picked up a hitchhiker on the way down to Miami, and I named him Sunshine. Sunshine and I became friends.

"We stopped at Disney World for a day on our way down. Sunshine and I separated from them at Disney World, and we did our own thing. We scored some acid and dropped it while we were still in the theme park. We were having a good trip, so to speak."

"Hold on for a minute Marsha," she said. I anticipated her question. "You took LSD?"

"Yes, I had tripped before but it wasn't something I did often."

"This wasn't your first time then?" she asked.

"No, but let me go on with my story." I wanted to stay on point and not get caught up in the drug issue. I knew most people who had never done drugs or knew anyone who had would get hung up on this part. The natural assumption would have been that I was in a drug-induced state. I knew I would be able to prove her wrong if I could continue.

"Go ahead, Marsha," she said.

I knew she wanted to bust me. She had many years of practicing her method of getting the truth out of her students. I knew she had heard every kind of story or excuse.

I continued. "When we left Disneyland, Sunshine told me that my friends, especially Kathy, were evil. I remember getting into the car and once inside, everything around me got dark. Yes, I was still tripping, but this was a darkness that engulfed my whole being. It begins on the outside, but it felt like it penetrated me within."

I paused and watched her. I tried to read her expression. She sat without expression.

I wanted to imitate her calmness and matter-of-fact coolness. I'm very expressive by nature, so it was difficult for me to speak without using my hands. I tried to control them as much as possible. Too many gestures might have made me look like I was trying to sensationalize it.

I started again. "The darkness was not only dark, but it was beyond the darkness of the night. It was a supernatural darkness that I can't explain. There was a coldness that I felt, not like a cold in wintertime, but a cold that can't be explained either."

She interrupted, "You're in a car driving to Miami doing LSD. You say your friend is evil. It's dark and cold, right?"

"Right."

"These are some very unusual things that seem to be happening to you, Marsha."

"Yep, I can say amen to that. It was very strange for me also. Somewhere in this journey I felt I was being pulled to a horrible place. What I experienced can't be expressed in words. The only way that I can attempt to explain that feeling was isolation from God. Of course, right now in the world, God is everywhere. He has not taken His hands or breath out of this world, not yet."

"Marsha, it sounds like you were having a bad trip and the LSD brought this on. I've seen several documentaries on people who doctors gave LSD to. They were studying the effects of it on their patients. Some of them saw pretty flowers and others saw nice things. Some said they had a wonderful time experiencing the drug. Still others screamed, cried, and said it was horrible and scary. They thought they saw monsters or demons. Some were never the same afterwards. These are scientific documentary studies performed by neurologists and scientists. You see, Marsha, LSD is a mind-altering drug."

I wasn't about to back down now. "I know this as well, and I have also watched some of those shows. But how do you explain those bites on my back that were seen by six people? My mother, my ten-year-old daughter, my aunt and uncle, my cousin who's a registered nurse, and my friend Mary, who has known me since we were nine years old. They were witnesses to the bites.

"Never once in any of those studies did any physical condition show up on those people. It was all about their mental health. Now I do know that in other countries like Africa or Haiti, they believe in demons and have experienced eerie, creepy, and unanswerable phenomena. We here in America think we are too sophisticated and too educated to believe in such things as demons."

What I had experienced was real. My only reason to tell this to her was to uplift Jesus. This was more for her than me. I was going to heaven. My concern was for her.

The atmosphere in the office quickly changed. I was now in charge, or should I say He was in charge. The evidence presented to her had surpassed her knowledge of what she thought she knew.

"Marsha, never in my life have I ever heard of anything like this. I really don't know how to respond to you. I don't want to say I don't believe you. However, I am not sure if I can agree this happened to you. You've given me something to think about."

I smiled. "The only thing I want you to think about is the reality of Jesus Christ. He is not just a good man that lived thousands of years ago. He is the only true and living God. He is the only way to heaven. There is a hell. You will end up there if you don't accept Him as a living Savior."

"Marsha, you're the only person I know who has such a passion for Jesus. I have to commend you on that. It has sure been interesting getting to know you and working with you. I have a list of students in my journals that made an impression on me. You will be added to that list."

She stood up and stretched out her hand to me. I quickly left my desk and extended my hand to her. We shook hands. I wanted to embrace her but knew that would have been inappropriate.

We let our eyes meet for a moment. I knew this was my cue to leave and return to my office.

As I walked back to my office, I asked the Lord to open her heart to let her know Him.

Chapter Twelve

REGRETFUL TO REJOICING

I was exhausted mentally trying to keep the family going I felt like a hamster running on a wheel going around and around, but not getting anywhere.

Rick's moods were forever changing. We never knew what would send him into a rage. His unpredictability made us feel as if we were always trying to maneuver through a minefield.

I took a weekend job as a cocktail waitress I definitely needed extra income. Rick and I had been married for over six years. I was only attending church once a month if that. I never quit reading my bible nor praying. I knew I could never allow myself to stop trusting the Lord, even in the middle of all my desperation. Jesus was my only friend.

One Friday night as I dressed to go to work, I knew Rick wasn't in the best of moods. I finished getting ready as quickly as I could.

I had taken the kids to the skating rink earlier that day. My mother had planned to pick them up, and then they would spend the night with her. Thankfully, the kids were not home with him this night.

Rick walked in the bedroom. I could tell by his demeanor he was angry.

I forced a smile on my face and tried to speak with a calm and even voice. "Well, I'm about ready to leave," I said, hoping my anxiety didn't show.

"Yeah, that's good for you, leaving me here by myself on a Friday night," he spat out.

"I can't help that. You know we need the extra money." I cringed inside, wishing I hadn't responded. I knew that when money was brought up, the situation would only turn ugly.

"Yeah, those are your kids, not mine, so you need to work for them," he said in a loud voice.

"You're right, and I'm supporting them and you too," I snapped back.

Then he said something to me which I will not repeat, but it cut me to the core. I left with tears in my eyes. His words reminded me of a terrible day long ago in the past. We had never discussed it. I buried it in a sea of regret, never to resurface. Evidently Rick had not.

Painful Memories

I had gotten pregnant three months after we got married. Neither one of us was prepared to bring a baby into the world. Rick mentioned about getting an abortion, which were illegal in 1971. Rick told me his friend knew a doctor in Georgia who performs abortions.

After several weeks, his friend finally made contact with this doctor. We drove for several hours with his friend to Georgia.

The location of the doctor's office was in a sleazy side of town. When we arrived at his office, I felt numb inside. All of this seemed surreal to me. At the time, I was married to a man I had not taken the time to know. I had blindly given into my emotions. I allowed Rick to manipulate me, and I was about to pay a very heavy price for it.

A man words can be very convincing to a woman. Especially her husband I was madly in love with him and he had made a strong argument about having a baby at this time. Really, I agreed that the timing was not right.

We hardly knew each other and there was no stability in our lives at all.

They say love is blind. I didn't consider this to be a cliché. I *was* blinded. I had exchanged the stability, provision, and leadership I had seen in my father and grandfather and settled for excitement, adventure, intrigue, and suspense.

Now I was about to walk into a strange doctor's office to have an abortion. What did an abortion entail? I had never known anyone who had one.

I kept silent as Rick held my hand. We entered the small storefront office of an old brick building.

When Rick opened the door to the doctor's office, it had that all too familiar smell. The modestly furnished waiting room consisted of old green leather chairs placed along the walls. End tables sat in each corner of the room with matching lamps on them. The old wall-to-wall brown carpet was worn from years of use. The pale green walls could have used a new coat of paint.

A faded sign behind a small glass window at the back of the room read "Please check in with receptionist."

We were the only ones there. Rick's friend walked to the receptionist's window and gently knocked on it.

Rick and I stood several feet away. The window opened after a few minutes. From where I stood, I couldn't see the lady talking behind the sliding window. I could hear the conversation though.

He told her we were from Jacksonville and that we had an appointment. He then turned around and motion for us to sit down.

I watched as he left the room. I assumed he went to the doctor's office.

Rick put his arm around me. I knew this was hard on him too.

He then told me that his friend was paying for the abortion but he had made arrangements to pay him back.

I didn't question him, and I didn't want to talk. I wasn't sure what I wanted. I felt empty of any emotion.

His friend opened the door and called us into the doctor's' office.

Rick still held my hand as we entered the room. The doctor was an older man with gray hair with a grandfather-like appearance.

He looked at me. "How far along are you?"

"I'm not sure. I haven't had a period for two possibly three months."

"Okay. Go to the third room and wait."

I felt so strange and scared. I hadn't seen any nurses, nor had I seen any patients. I hadn't even seen the receptionist.

The hallway had an eerie silence to it. I expected a monster or something evil to pop out of one of the rooms.

I entered the third room. It looked like a regular examination room except that all the equipment was old. Everything in his whole office was outdated.

I sat on the examination bed, fully clothed. I didn't have to wait long before the doctor walked in.

He said, "You'll need to undress." He then handed me a gown, but he didn't leave the room.

I asked, "Where can I go to change?"

"Right here."

"Do you have a bathroom?"

"Yes, but change here in this room."

I felt so uncomfortable and began to feel faint. Again, I told him I needed to go to the bathroom and wanted my husband.

The doctor pointed me to the bathroom. I didn't care that it was a small, drab, and unclean. I was grateful for the privacy.

I shuddered. I felt overwhelmed, helpless, and flat-out terrified. It was like I was the main character in a horror movie.

I was alone, really alone. Where was Rick? Was I being self-centered? What was Rick feeling? He was young. He had never been married, but now he had a family with three small children. I knew he loved me but I had so many strange emotions swirling around in my head.

I walked back to the examination room with my clothes in one hand, and I used my other hand to hold my gown together in the back. The old doctor told me to get on the bed and turn onto my side. I watched him as he prepared two shots.

He didn't say anything but gave both shots on one side of my buttocks.

He said, "Don't move," and then he walked out.

I lay there wondering what to expect next. It seemed like I had stayed on my side for about fifteen minutes.

The doctor entered the room. "Get up and get dressed," he said, staring at me. "You can dress in the room."

I said, "No, I'll dress in the bathroom." A creepy, yucky feeling came over me. I wanted to cuss him out, but I knew that would only make this day worse.

I walked back to the bathroom and dressed. I left the gown on the unclean floor. I washed my hands in the sink, and the cold water felt good to me. I splashed some water on my face, hoping that I could wash off that dirty feeling.

I headed back to the waiting room, where Rick and his friend were waiting. Rick put his arm around me, trying to comfort me.

The doctor talked to our friend like they had known each other for a long time. They acted like nothing had happened, just another day in the neighborhood. This wasn't my neighborhood, though.

I wanted to say something but I decided not to say anything for fear of what would come spewing out of my mouth.

Our friend made the comment that we had a four-hour drive back and needed to leave. He shook hands with the doctor and thanked him. Rick didn't shake the doctor's hand but kept his arm around me.

I was puzzled, wondering how our friend knew about this doctor, especially since he lived in another state. I was sure I was not the first girl he had brought here.

Later that week, Rick let me in on a secret. He told me that his friend had not wanted him to marry me, or anyone else for that matter. His friend's house was the party house where I first met Rick.

I guess I put a damper on his fun. Before we got married, people dropped in to hear the music and do drugs, but that all stopped after we got married.

When Rick told him I was pregnant, he told Rick it would be the end of his music career. He didn't need a wife, much less a child.

His boss had paid for the band's equipment and acted as their manager. Rick had never had a father figure, so this friend somewhat filled that role. He was at least twenty years older than Rick and had given him a place to live. All of this influenced Rick's decision and mine too.

Two weeks after we visited the doctor, I woke up with some cramping and bleeding. I decided to go to work, though, thinking I could take something for the pain. Since I was a young girl, I'd always had bad cramps with my periods. Sometimes the cramps were so bad, they caused me to vomit. I knew this wasn't my normal period, but I didn't think it would be much different.

I continued my morning routine, getting the kids their cereal and milk. DeAnna was going to kindergarten. Ricky and Scotty stayed home with Rick. He was my babysitter, which saved me money.

While getting dressed, the cramps got worse. I felt very strange and lightheaded. I sat down on the toilet and out gushed a lot of dark red and thick blood. I doubled over in pain. The room swirled. I tried to call for Rick but couldn't speak.

I felt like I was about to faint. I got very nauseous and begin to sweat. The pain was excruciating. I began to lose consciousness.

I tried to call Rick again. I bent over so far that my head almost touched the floor.

Rick came in. I could tell he was frightened. He picked me up and took me to the bedroom. Thank God, the kids were not aware of what was happening.

He called my mother to come and watch the kids. He told her I was sick. I hadn't told her about the abortion.

Rick then called my friend Gwen to take us to the hospital. I was in and out of consciousness because of blood loss and the pain.

When Mom arrived, she immediately wanted to call an ambulance. Rick reassured her that he had everything under control and that help was on the way.

Mom kissed me on my forehead. "What happened?"

Rick said, "She's having a very bad period."

Mom immediately took charge of the kids, reassuring them that their mother would be okay. I was relieved knowing she was there with them. Gwen got to the house, and Rick carried me to her car.

I felt the blood pouring down my legs. Gwen drove extremely fast, running red lights and racing down 8th Street to St. Luke's Hospital, about five miles from our house. She quickly pulled in front of the emergency room.

Rick grabbed me out of the backseat. He rushed me into the ER screaming, "I need a doctor."

Nurses rushed around me and instructed Rick where to take me.

He carried me to a room with a large bright light. I could hear the nurses and a doctor call my name several times.

I heard one nurse say, "Her blood pressure is sixty over forty."

I felt so light I thought I was floating. It felt so weird. A nurse put an oxygen mask on me and started giving me shots.

After a few minutes, the severe pain left me. I felt so relaxed I wanted to sleep, but one of the nurses kept talking to me. She said, "Don't go to sleep." She wiped my forehead with a cold rag.

My feet had been placed in stirrups as if I was having a baby. I wondered why.

I thought after an abortion you would just start your period. That's what that doctor told me. Rick's friend told me the same thing. Rick told me that he knew of several girls who had gone to the same doctor, and they had no trouble afterwards. That is when I knew with certainty that his boss had done this before.

The ER doctor asked, "How are you feeling?"

"Much better," I murmured.

He said, "When we get you stabilized, we'll let your husband come back."

I saw bloody sheets in the corner of the room, and the bright light in the ceiling had been turned off.

The doctor left after patting my arm.

I was still unsure what had happened to me. My mind was fuzzy, and I knew it must have been because of those shots they gave me. I wanted to see Rick and get some answers.

One of the nurses said, "Your husband's on his way."

When Rick came back, the nurses left. It was just the two of us. He kissed me, and he had tears in his eyes.

"I'm better," I said. "I want to go home."

He walked over to the counter, staring down into a large round aluminum basin.

"Rick," I repeated, "I want to go home."

He turned to face me. Tears ran down his checks. He picked up the basin with both hands and brought it to me.

He said, "Marsha, here is our son."

"What?" was all I could say. My mind couldn't comprehend what he had said.

Inside that basin was a very tiny baby boy. He had sprigs of blonde hair and long legs. I couldn't believe what I was looking at. I could feel hot tears streaming down my cheeks. This was not at all what I had expected.

I couldn't breathe. I gasped to catch my breath.

Rick just kept looking into the basin as he carried it back to the counter. The doctor came in with an administrator to talk with us.

They asked, "What do you want done with the fetus?"

I cried, "Fetus? What's a fetus? I had never heard that word before.

The doctor didn't answer my question. Instead, he said, "The hospital can take care of it for you."

I couldn't say anything. Rick signed a paper and walked out of the room.

The doctor said, "You lost a lot of blood, so we'll be admitting you."

I stayed in the hospital for a week.

October 23

All those past memories flooded back in like a tidal wave. Why did Rick have to remind me of that which I had kept locked away? I quickly finished getting ready for work. I knew if I opened my mouth, I was going to say things that I could never take back and it scared me to think what may have come out of my mouth.

Of all times, after six years, why did he bring up that painful memory? And what he said concerning it was even more painful. How dare he say something so awful to me concerning that day? It was so hurtful it brought back all the shame and guilt.

Rick and I had never talked about it since that day in the hospital. It was too painful and shameful for both of us. I couldn't believe he went as low as he did with the statement he made to me.

He pushed my buttons that night because, unbeknown to him, I was pregnant again. Several weeks before, I put my birth-control pills in my pocketbook to remind myself to get a refill. While driving across the bridge on the way to work that night, I had a change of heart. I reached into my purse and flung my pills out the window. I kept what I had done a secret.

When I discovered I was pregnant, I had mixed feelings. There was a sense of excitement but, at the same time, I was scared.

The next week, after that terrible night, I told Rick I was pregnant.

Rick was elated. I knew we had uncertainty concerning our future. Knowing that he was going to have a baby caused him to immerse himself in his music more than ever.

I started going to a neighborhood clinic, where they assigned me a midwife named Teresa. I was thirty years old and hadn't been pregnant in eight years.

Some days I was ecstatic over being pregnant. Other times, an overwhelming feeling of fear gripped me because I knew my life would be changing again. I feared the worst but prayed for the best.

DeAnna was thirteen and was thrilled at the possibility of having a baby sister. She had always wanted a little sister. When Ricky was born, she went to the doctor with me for his six-week checkup. When the doctor came into the room, she immediately told the doctor to take him back and get her a sister. The doctor laughed and told her she would have to be a big sister to her brother.

Ricky and Scotty were nine and eight years old now. As boys, they didn't act too excited, but I knew they were.

Over the nine months of my pregnancy, my emotions went up and down like a yo-yo.

On October 23, I awoke feeling more pressure than usual. I went to the bathroom, and my water broke.

I had been pregnant three times, and never once had my water broke. I just stood there for a couple of seconds.

Rick was in the kitchen, and I called for him.

"Yeah?" he called back. "I'm making my coffee."

"We need to go the hospital. My water just broke."

As we stepped outside, the cool air felt fresh. I glanced around and noticed how the azaleas in the neighborhood looked radiant in the morning light. Their pink flowers seemed to be saying, "Good morning." Everything was good, and I was happy.

I thanked the Lord for morning labor. All my other births occurred during the early morning and late-night hours. This baby was going to be born in the daytime.

After checking into the hospital, a nurse brought me a wheelchair.

I said, "I'm able to walk to the labor and delivery ward."

She said, "Hospital rules. You have to be in the wheelchair."

Rick stayed close by my side. Off we rolled to the labor and delivery floor.

My midwife, Teresa, greeted me. She had already delivered another baby earlier that morning. She took us to the labor room that was directly across from the nurse's station.

"Teresa?" I asked. "Can I walk instead of staying in here?" I put my hands on my stomach.

She looked at me with one raised eyebrow. "You want to walk?"

I tried to smile. "I just don't want to be in a bed right now."

"Well, okay. Most women who are in labor want to have an epidural to ease the pain." Her right eyebrow remained raised.

I quickly replied, "I want to try to have the baby naturally."

She handed me two hospital gowns. "Be sure to put the extra gown on to cover your naked butt," she said with a chuckle. "Marsha, check back in with me. Don't have that baby in the waiting area."

"No," I smiled back. "I won't do that. I promise."

I remembered being in labor with DeAnna. I was young, scared, and just turned eighteen three weeks prior to her birth. I had heard horror stories of labor. So, when I felt my first really hard contractions, I called the nurse begging for something. Of course, she knew it was more my fear than pain but she came back with a shot, that put me in a "twilight sleep." I had no memory of anything, until I woke up to a beautiful baby girl with a head full of dark hair.

Three years later, I got pregnant with Ricky. I had a very difficult labor that lasted three days. My doctor told me never to get pregnant again.

But I did. I got pregnant nine months later with Scotty. My labor with him was only two hours, but it was very hard. They didn't allow me to hold Scotty after he was born. They rushed him to the neonatal care unit. After twelve hours, they brought him to me. Thank God, he checked out fine.

I decided I wanted to have this baby naturally. It had been eight years since I had given birth. I was older, more mature, and obviously experienced in childbirth. More importantly, I knew Jesus.

Rick walked beside me as I waddled out into the waiting room area, where families anticipated the arrival of their new family members. I was the only expectant mother out there.

My stroll didn't last long, because my labor increased. The pains came faster, and I had to stop walking each time I had a contraction.

I had never attended any classes for natural childbirth, but I knew it was time to go back into the labor room.

Teresa sat at the nurse's station doing paperwork. She smiled as she saw us.

She was a middle-aged lady who had been my midwife during the whole term of my pregnancy. I was glad she was on duty this morning. I trusted her.

I went back to my room and climbed into bed, or should I say scooted with Rick's help. Teresa checked on me to find out how many centimeters I had dilated.

She smiled after her examination, and said, "Wow! Marsha, you're already at eight centimeters."

My labor pains had intensified. I quickly decided I didn't want natural childbirth after all and made that very clear to Teresa.

She smiled. "Well, Marsha, you never attended a Lamaze class, and you just made a quick decision without preparing yourself. Yes, that was me.

I watched as one of the nurses started an IV on the top of my hand.

Rick started humming *Amazing Grace*. The acoustics in the room turned out to be very good. He went from humming the song to singing in a low voice.

I don't think he realized that his voice had carried outside my room into the hallway. I heard other voices joining in. It was two black nurses who were sitting at the nurse's station in front of my room.

Teresa walked back in with a needle. "Marsha, I'm going to give you some Demerol to ease your labor."

She inserted the Demerol into my IV line, and immediately my pain level went from ten to seven. Oh, the sweet relief!

I thanked her. Then the fetal monitor hooked to my stomach began to beep.

"Oh no! We're putting the baby to sleep!" Teresa said as she dashed out of the room.

A couple moments later, she injected another shot into my IV.

BOOM!

That excruciating pain was back in full force. Now I was forced to have natural childbirth.

Within the hour, I was being pushed into the delivery room. Rick stood over me. There was a mirror overhead so I could watch the birth. The nurse placed my feet into the stirrups.

I reached up to grab Rick's strong arms, which he had placed on each side of my head. Each time Teresa told me to push, I grabbed his arms and pushed with all my might.

I watched the clock for thirty-five minutes. All I heard was, "Push. Stop. Now push. Stop." I was exhausted and still in pain.

Teresa's voice became serious. "Marsha, you have to get this baby out now."

I somehow gained the strength, and I pushed and pulled to the point that Rick was actually straining as he pulled against the force of my pull. In the overhead mirror, I could see the top of my baby's head.

Another two or three pushes, and out came a beautiful baby girl. She weighed eight pounds, eight ounces. She was my biggest baby, and we named her Erika Eve.

On that morning, the Yarbrough's added another one to its clan.

Chapter Thirteen

THE DREAM

What an unusual dream!

I wasn't sure whether I should share it with Rick though. I dreamed about a musician that I had never personally met. He was the lead singer of a band that had started in Jacksonville, Florida and had grown to fame.

I knew Rick was as talented but had not achieved the recognition as this band had. I wasn't sure how Rick would react to me dreaming about another musician. The dream stayed with me for a week before I finally decided it was the right time to share it.

One of the band's songs came on radio. I knew I had to choose my words carefully Rick was so unpredictable, he could change without warning.

"Wow! I had a dream about Ronnie VanZant. How weird is that?"

"It was a strange dream, though," I continued, "I was in a jeep, or an ATV in a swampy area. I looked down and crawling out of the swamp was Ronnie VanZant. I reached out to him to help him on to the jeep. He was dirty and muddy.

"I then drove him to a church. I stood at the back of the church and watched him as he walked down the aisle and gave his life to Jesus Christ."

I braced myself for his response.

He just said, "Really?" and didn't make any other comments.

A week after I had told Rick about my dream, their plane crashed October 20, 1977 which killed Ronnie VanZant, Steve and Cassie Gaines, who were brother and sister, their two pilots and their road manager, Dean Kilpatrick. The news only reported that they had crashed after running out of fuel near a small town in Mississippi.

The Call

Rick's band was playing on the weekends. He came home all excited and woke me up. "Marsha!" Tonight, I met a guy in the club who said, he was one of the roadies for Lynyrd Skynyrd, and asked for my number.

Half awake, I said "Really?" What ran through my thoughts were people claimed to be somebody they're not. However, not wanting to sound negative, I smiled and hugged him.

He hugged me back and left the bedroom, silently I whispered to the Lord, "Let this be real." I hadn't been to church in a while, however I was still reading my Bible daily. I was hanging onto Jesus more than ever, all I had was Jesus.

I was washing dishes and the phone rang, I called for Rick to answer it but he didn't. As usual I dropped what I was doing and hurried to the phone.

"Hello," I said.

A male's voice asked, "May I speak to Rick Yarbrough? This is Allen Collins with the Lynyrd Skynyrd Band."

I wanted to say, "Sure it is." Instead I yelled, "Rick?"

He came out of the bedroom. I didn't tell him who was on the phone. I stayed within earshot to hear the conversation.

It only took a few minutes of listening, and I knew it was indeed Allen Collins.

Allen asked if he could meet him. He invited Rick out to his home since he was still recovering from the plane crash. Allen gave his address and asked if he could come Friday night. They continued their conversation, I heard Rick telling Allen he had written a song about the band after the crash. Allen said yes, he wanted to hear it.

Friday night couldn't get here fast enough. Rick nervously chatted away as I was inwardly praising the Lord, as I drove us to what I was thinking this is an answer to pray.

When we arrived, we were greeted warmly by Allen, his wife Kathy, and their two young daughters Amie and Allison. Allen and Rick went towards the den and Kathy and I went to the kitchen.

She offered me some sweet tea as we the usual small talk getting acquainted. The kitchen was within ear and eye view of the den, and both of us tried not to eavesdrop on the guys, but we were curious.

It wasn't long we heard a guitar sound. It was Allen. Kathy looked surprised and with tears in her eyes, she said, "That's the first time since the crash that he's picked up his guitar. The doctors thought they were going to have to amputate his arm due to the extent of his injury."

Allen sat in his recliner, while Rick sat on the couch. Rick called out the chords of the song he had had written, and Allen strummed them.

After Allen and Rick finished with the song, Kathy and I joined them in the den.

I asked Allen, "Can you tell me about the crash?"

He said that the plane ran out of fuel. The pilots tried to land on a small airstrip, but the plane ended up crashing into a wooded area surrounded by swampland. This made it hard for rescue vehicles to get to them. The rescuers had to use ATV's and pickup trucks. Six people had died. Allen fought back his tears as he told the story.

After he finished, I told them about my dream. I knew then the Lord had given me that dream. Before we left that night, I knew this was a beginning of a friendship. Allen asked Rick to come back so they could talk more about their music. This was an answer to prayer.

Within weeks, we were accepted like family. Rick and Allen stayed busy writing music. Kathy and I watched our daughters play. Finally, our days of struggling seemed to be coming to an end. I fantasized about moving into a nice home, the kids having nice things, and not stressing out over money. I looked forward to quitting my job at the temporary agency that I took just to keep us afloat.

Often Allen and Rick would write late into the night. Kathy went upstairs to bed, and I'd catnap on the couch in the den. When Allen got the hungry, he would leave Rick in the studio, which was located behind their house. He headed to the kitchen, opened a can of fruit cocktail, and pour its contents into a large bowl, adding extra cherries.

He'd yell, "Marsha, you want some fruit cocktail?"

Then he usually lit a joint, pass it to me, and hand me a spoon.

We both ate out of the same bowl, trying to beat each other to the next bite. I began to talk about the Lord with him. At times he would bring out their large family Bible and ask me about the book of Revelation.

I tried to explain those scriptures the best I could. I had remembered some of them from my childhood.

Allen was curious about the end-times and was open and enjoyed our time of reading the Bible together. There we sat, smoking a joint, eating fruit cocktail with a large family Bible on the kitchen table, talking about God.

Reforming the Band

Allen and Gary wanted to reform the band. They chose the name The Rossington Collins Band or RCB as they called it. It was a combination of Gary's and Allen's last names.

Both Gary and Allen included Rick when talking about putting a band together. All three of them had spent two years working and writing songs together.

When one of the producers from MCA Records came to Jacksonville to discuss the band's rebirth, they decided they didn't want to compare RCB to Lynyrd Skynyrd. They said Rick looked too much like Ronnie VanZant, with his long blonde hair and southern voice. They thought it best for RCB to have a new image.

So, Dale Krantz became their lead vocalist. She was just right for the group, and since she was female, no one could compare them to the Lynyrd Skynyrd band.

The band produced two albums. When Rick was told that MCA had decided not to include him, he was devastated. I knew Allen and Gary were unhappy about this decision but needed to do what was best for the band. Rick had spent a lot of time with both of them, and they had formed a bond, this was equally hard on both Allen and Gary.

They all remained friends, though. Rick continued to write and put together another band. I started working for a friend of mine that managed a convenience store.

Welcome, Jasmine Faith

Having my expectations shot down again, I cried and whined to the Lord but kept repeating my usual go to verse *all things work together for good, for those that love the Lord*. I had not noticed, I had missed my period for two months. I was certain I was not pregnant though, as a teenager that was common for me. I blamed it on stress.

Finally, I decided to go to the clinic. After the Dr. examines me, he said I had fibroid tumors. He told me if my period didn't start by next month he would recommend surgery. I had mixed emotions, although I hadn't planned to have another baby, I didn't want to have surgery either. I made another appointment before leaving which was four weeks away.

My appointment day came so I brought a book to pass the time *A God Kind of Faith*. The wait at the clinic was usually an all-day event.

I prayed I would be able to trust the Lord without question. I prayed for my faith to increase and asked for faith like Abraham and the other biblical characters I had read about.

"Marsha," the nurse called my name.

I closed my book and followed her back to one of the exam rooms. She handed me a gown and asked me to change, assuring me that the doctor would be in shortly. She handed me a paper cup and asked me to pee in it. I returned from the restroom, handed the cup back to her, and walked back to the room. I continued to read my book.

Several minutes later, three men walked in. I knew the two younger-looking ones were still interns and the older one was the lead doctor.

The doctor told me, "Your chart indicates you might have to have surgery. Have you had your period since your last visit?"

"No, I answered.

I watched his eyes as he glanced quickly over my chart. He handed my chart to one of the interns and in doctor dialogue they discussed something about false negatives pregnancy tests. He asked the nurse to bring in a fetal monitor.

He then proceeded to perform that dreaded exam most women hate, and then he placed the fetal monitor on my flat stomach. I heard that all-too-familiar sound of a baby's heartbeat.

"You're pregnant," he announced.

I was unprepared for his statement. I was not having surgery, but a baby!

I was relieved and scared at the same time. That book *a God Kind of Faith* I was going to have to walk it now. I had no other one to trust but God.

So many different emotions would charge through me. Fear and excited of expecting another child seem to fight each other. Fear would say you can barely feed the children you have now, what you will do with another baby. Than my mother's natural instincts of having a baby again would make me smile. Those nine months went by fast. The night I went into labor, DeAnna and Rick were discussing the baby's name. If this baby was a girl, her first name would be Jasmine.

Rick wanted her middle name to be Jam, like musicians jamming.

DeAnna said, "Dad, everyone will be calling her Jelly instead."

I listened but said nothing. I knew exactly what her middle name would be Faith.

I finally let both know that we could settle on the middle name later on, or I was going to have this baby at home.

Within two hours of arriving at the hospital, Jasmine Faith was born. She weighed eight pounds, twelve ounces. She had brown hair and large brown eyes. She was a beautiful, long-legged baby.

Still Moving on with Music

Rick never stopped his dream about making it in music, music was his life. He had put bands together and recorded songs in a well-known studio in Miami. He played all around the state. We continued to keep in touch with Allen and Kathy, though. Allen stayed on the road with RCB most of the time and I talked mainly to Kathy over the phone. When Allen was off the road, he and Rick would end up in a studio working together on one of Rick's original songs. Allen would do most of the lead guitar work for him.

Billboard Magazine did a small article on Rick. Rick had sent demos to some music producers in California and two of them came to Florida to sign him to a music contract. Our expectations would rise again. Than within weeks we would get a phone call saying that producer was fired or something else had happened to stop it. I accused God of dangling a carrot in front of us just to take it away. What game was God playing? Rick was hurt and disappointed too. He did not know how to handle his pain of rejection and it came out in unhealthy ways which made my life and the kids terrible at times. But he never gave up though on his music and I still felt like I needed to support him.

One Sunday at church, I ran into a friend, who lived across the street from Allen and Kathy.

He asked, "Have you talked to Kathy since Allen's been on the road touring with the band?"

I said, " Not since last week."

"Would you mind calling her? She seems a little depressed."

I assured him I would. I knew Kathy was in her early stages of pregnancy.

The next day I did as I promised, but no one answered so I left a message. I then called her mother's house but no answer either.

Several days later, while heading to the store I hear on the radio that Kathy Collins, wife of Allen Collins, had died suddenly.

I turned my car around and headed back home. A person close to the family had called Rick and he was crying. We prayed for

Allen, Allison, and Amie, and their families. Rick left immediately for their home.

Rick stayed close to Allen for several years after Kathy's death, but Allen never fully recovered. Allen just hid his pain in drugs and alcohol.

Unfortunately, due to a car accident that killed Allen's girlfriend, he ended up paralyzed and in a wheelchair. Allen died on January 23, 1990 and was buried next to Kathy.

Rick continued writing and recording his songs. He got one offer after another from different promoters promising this and that but they could never deliver.

It was as if someone was taunting us. The prize was always within reach but snatched away each time. Hurt, bitterness, and pain were mounting, which forced me to trust Jesus deeper, even though I had so many questions. I had to fight not to allow bitterness and strife to come into my heart.

Even though I didn't understand why this was happening, I tried to encourage myself and the kids with my favorite go-to scripture, Romans 8:28: "All things work for the best to those that are called of God and love Him."

Trust Jesus was my catchphrase, but I had to climb over my own mountains of doubts, fears and disappointments too.

I fought back the feelings of anger although I just did not know who to be angry at.

Chapter Fourteen

MARSHA'S GHOST

Struggling to pay bills or just having the daily necessities was so common, like putting on my shoes each morning. Money was always at the center of my life, or I should I say no money. I had taken a job across town at a department store. I had no car and had to take two buses. My shifts rotated weekly, from day shift to night shift. Changing buses downtown at night and walking home from the bus stop, kept me on high alert but I found the Lord was ever presence. The department store went out of business and I was left without a job, again.

Rick continued writing songs, but now focused more on Christian songs. Christian rock had arrived as a new genre, and Christian radio stations were becoming more popular.

The Holy Spirit at times would bring back to my memory what He had spoken to me years earlier. I quoted those words out loud and reminded my children of His promise. "Keep your eyes off the church. Keep your eyes off of man. My children won't come to me. I will go to them. It will be bigger and better and nationwide."

I knew when the Holy Spirit spoke about the Church, He was not referring to those believers, who had a personal relationship but those who misrepresented the grace and mercy of Jesus. Who wanted to present God as an authoritative bully and controlled the people with fear and manipulation. It was more of them being religious wanting the approval of men not the Lord. Jesus had the same problem with the self- righteous men, he called them snakes and vapors.

My prayer was, "Lord, use Rick and his music, so we can go into the entire world telling everyone about Jesus."

I envisioned Rick would sing about the Lord, and I would tell everyone about this great Savior with whom I had fallen in love with.

During this time DeAnna had graduated and married her high-school sweetheart Mike Adamson. They had a very small wedding at his house. I was happy for them. Mike's family fell in love with her and her them.

I knew DeAnna had the potential to achieve much more than she realized. She wasn't just beautiful and smart, but she possessed strong leadership qualities. She had been such a blessing to me. I really felt her absence.

Again, I was job hunting and saw an opening in a pawn shop. I applied in person and was hired on the spot. The shop was located at 8th and Main Street, which was nicknamed pawn shop row. Pawns shops lined both sides of the street. At one time, it had been a very upscale neighborhood. But as it goes in most cities, older neighborhoods eventually become a thing of the past, and Main Street had become just that.

Pawn shops had become popular not only with people who needed fast money but also with some of the middle-class and professional people. They found that they could haggle on the prices making it more interesting.

I really enjoyed my job. I met all sorts of unique people and learned quickly not to judge a book by its cover. The pawn-shop district was located in a less-than-desirable part of town. You absolutely didn't want to be there after dark.

One day on my lunch hour, I stepped out the back door of the shop just to be ordered back in by a loud voice. "Stay back."

Later, I learned that SWAT was in a standoff with local drug dealers, who had set up their drug houses behind the shops. You never knew what to expect over the course of an eight-hour day. As a result, my life at the pawn shop was never boring.

Let Me Introduce You to a Gift of the Spirit

When the owner first hired me, the employees told me strange stories about our shop being haunted. I listened to them but didn't think much about it.

I had only been working there a couple of months when I had to retrieve a guitar. We kept the music equipment in our loft at the back of the shop. We hung the guitars that did not have a case by the same kind of wire used for a clothesline. Those in guitar cases were stacked up on the wall vertically leaning against each other.

I walked to the back of the store, turned on the light, and headed up the stairs. I had done this routine many times before, but this time was different. When I stepped onto the loft's floor it felt extremely cold. Strangely enough, this room didn't have any windows or openings to the outside, so I couldn't explain this unusual cold.

An eerie yet familiar feeling came over me. I knew I was in the presence of an evil spirit.

I said out loud, "I rebuke you in the name of Jesus!"

I felt a little uneasy. It had been a while since I had faced any demon. I retrieved the guitar and quickly exited the loft. I didn't feel comfortable sharing my experience, so I kept quiet.

We hired a new employee named Stacy, who was shy, quiet and kept to herself. I liked her immediately. After some small talk, my first question to her was "Do you know Jesus?"

She answered "Yes, I'm a Catholic."

I said, "No. I asked if you knew Jesus, not what religion you are."

I began to talk to her about Jesus. She was very receptive, and I knew she wanted to know more. Each day I would tell her a little bit more about the Holy Spirit. She would question me intensely. I knew she wanted to know more.

One morning when she came to work, she did not seem like herself.

"Stacy, what's wrong?" I asked.

She told me what she had experienced the previous night. She heard someone in her living room chanting, but she was home alone because her police officer husband was working.

She walked into her living room and saw a group of people. They walked around a star-like shape on the floor and were chanting something.

I immediately knew she was describing a pentagram, but she didn't even know what a pentagram was. I questioned her some more about this experience. She was completely innocent and baffled at what she had seen and heard. She had experienced her first vision, but she didn't know it.

I told her about the power of Jesus blood and the power in the name of Jesus that she could use against any demonic activity. I explained that in His name, demons have to leave, and Satan has to bow.

Over the next couple of weeks, she asked me many questions. I told her what I knew from the Bible and what I had experienced.

I said, "Ask the Holy Spirit to reveal and confirm the truth to you."

I knew in my spirit that Stacy was going to be used by God. Her innocence, along with her humility, made her a splendid candidate for Jesus.

Her prayers were being answered quickly. I was amazed at how the Holy Spirit showed her all of these spiritual things so fast. She was teachable, hungry and very cautious concerning this new walk. She reminded me of myself years ago.

I asked, "Stacey, will you go to church with me?"

She said, "No."

I knew she was scared to go. I asked God to take away her fear of going to another church besides a Catholic one. I kept talking to her about praying in the Spirit. I wanted to share about the gift of tongues with her, and unbeknownst to me, she had already asked God to confirm if speaking in tongues were real.

Stacy and I were doing inventory at the shop, which put us working together for a week. I explained to her about the gift of praying in the spirit, using scriptures, and she listened intently.

However, she was very concerned that she would be cursing God if she spoke in tongues.

She asked, "Is this the devil's language or God's?"

I reassured her that the devil had no part in this wonderful gift. I said, "There's a Christian radio station, and all week they've been teaching about the gift of tongues, and I know it'll answer some of your questions."

I thanked God that His timing was so perfect, that He loved Stacy enough to confirm what we had been discussing in the back of a pawn shop through a radio station. I marveled again that nothing was hidden from the Lord. He knew all our conversations.

Not long afterward, I knew the Lord wanted Stacy to come to church. Up to that point, she had managed to stay as far away as possible from my church.

I sensed the Holy Spirit wanting Stacy to come to church with me for our Wednesday night service. When we went to lunch, I told her what I felt. At the time she was attending nightly cosmetology school and had a big test. She couldn't miss it. I understood her not wanting to miss her test, but I had a strong sense that she needed to be at church though. I continued to pray, asking the Lord to speak to Stacy about coming to church tonight.

Rick called me at the shop, which was rare. "The Lord told me to call you and tell your friend Stacy she needed to come to church tonight."

This shocked me. Rick had never done anything like this before. I had told him very little about Stacy, I think the most I told him was that she was a Catholic, but I had been talking to her about Jesus.

I then told Stacy what God said to Rick. I could see in her eyes that she questioned the reality of my words and felt this was a conspiracy to get her to go to church.

She finally realized that neither Rick nor I had planned this, so she agreed to come with us. At the time, we attended New Covenant Ministries with Pastors Wiley and Jenna Tomlinson.

When all three of us walked into the sanctuary, I felt the atmosphere charged with His Presence. From Stacy's expression, I discerned that this was way out of her comfort zone. I knew this was a divine appointment.

We were scheduled to have a guest speaker, but Pastor Wiley believed the Holy Spirit wanted him to speak instead. He explained that during his prayer time, the Holy Spirit wanted him to teach on speaking in tongues.

I smiled, knowing God was at work. Not only was this for Stacy's benefit, but for mine as well.

As he began his lesson, he repeated verbatim what I had said. He also repeated the questions Stacy asked, whether she would be cursing God if she spoke in tongues.

Stacy was shaken, accusing me of recording our conversations and giving them to the pastor, however, she soon realized that wasn't possible because she had been with me the whole day. I worshipped God with uplifted hands, thanking Him who hears the very desires of our heart.

The pastor asked those who wanted to be filled with the Holy Spirit with the evidence of praying in tongues to come to the front. Stacy and I both walked to the front, where I laid my hands on her. She received her prayer language instantly. She still had some doubts, but I knew in His timing, the Holy Spirit would answer all her doubts with His Truth.

Things That Go Bump in the Day

I still hadn't told anyone what I had experienced with that evil spirit. The shop was busy and I needed Stacy to go redeem a guitar. After returning with the guitar, I noticed a strange look on her face. I asked if she was ok. She told me when I had time she wanted to talk with me. I took care of the customers, then I asked Stacy what was wrong. She told me when she entered the loft the air was thick and bone-chilling cold.

She felt fear, and two of the middle guitar cases fell as if someone had deliberately pushed them over. The end guitar cases stayed in their positions.

She said a dark shadow of a man wearing a top hat appeared. She immediately said, "In the name of Jesus, you have to leave."

Instantly the evil spirit left, and the atmosphere changed. She was stunned at what she had just experienced. She knew that that an evil presence had manifested.

I talked her into going back to the loft with me. She reluctantly agreed. I climbed the stairs, with Stacy close behind me.

Once inside, I saw the guitar cases on the ground just as she had said. I knew she'd had an encounter with and evil spirit, what she fondly named 'Marsha's ghost'.

We hired a young married couple, Denny and Theresa, we added to our pawn shop family. We were extremely busy on

Saturdays which left me up front overseeing the shop. I was the manager and the only one authorized to run the register also I okayed all the sales and pawns.

I sent Denny to the loft to redeem one of the pawns.

"Marsha, Marsha, can you help me, I can't find this merchandise!" I heard Denny's voice calling from the back, but he sounded different.

Because of the number of customers, I couldn't take the time to answer him back at this time. I thought what was wrong. Denny knew where all the merchandise was since he was our stockman. This was unlike him.

"Marsha, Marsha!" He called my name again but he hadn't moved an inch. The procedure for not finding the merchandise was to return to the pawn book and check the location, which we always wrote down.

He was a good worker, and I wondered why he didn't come to check the pawn book. I turned around to motion for him to come to me.

Denny was very pale, and his eyes were opened wide. I knew immediately something was wrong. I thought he had broken something valuable.

I left the pawn counter and register to find out what was wrong. He walked toward the staircase that led to the loft.

"Marsha, there is someone up there in the loft. I saw a man or something, and it's so cold up there. I can't go up there again. Please call the police. He may be dangerous or something."

Stacy walked back to see if she could help but saw Denny's expression, and immediately knew what had happened.

"Hey, Denny, did you meet Marsha's ghost?" she asked. "All you need to say is I rebuke you in the name of Jesus, and it will go." She smiled and left.

I asked Denny to follow me up to the loft.

"No," he said.

"Denny, you can do the same as Stacy did."

Denny said, "I'm not holy enough to say that."

I laughed. "Neither am I. It's not whether we're good or holy but because of what Jesus did for us on the cross. His blood made us righteous."

I smiled at Denny and told him how much Jesus loved him. I explained that we had no authority in ourselves but in Jesus name. He still was confessing that he wasn't holy and had not been to church in years. I put my arm around him reassuring him that nobody was holy so he was just like the rest of us. I reiterated that Jesus was not concern with him being holy but wanted him to have a personal relationship with him, instead.

The Ghosts Weren't Just in the Loft

We rented several rooms above the shop which were only accessible by going outside. Those rooms were used when we needed extra storage space.

We always kept the outside door locked, since it was right on the sidewalk. The walk up the narrow stairs made it difficult at times to retrieve or put pawns up.

One afternoon, Ralph, who co-owned another shop, had stopped in for a visit. While we discussed the business of the day, we heard a sound from upstairs that sounded like a trunk being dragged across the floor.

Ralph immediately looked up at the ceiling. "Marsha, you've got someone up there. We better go up and check it out."

I grabbed the key, and we both headed upstairs. He had his pistol with him. All pawnbrokers carried and had concealed weapon permits.

As soon as we reached the second floor, we headed in the direction of the sound.

We realized the sound had come from one of the rooms that were not ours. Therefore, I had no key to that room. There was a small glass window over the door.

Ralph was sure he'd heard someone in that room. He grabbed the ladder we always kept in the hallway, climbed to the top, and looked through the window. He stood there for a while. I watched as he carefully surveyed the room.

He gazed down at me with a puzzled look. "Marsha, I know I heard someone up here. You heard what sounded like someone dragging something across the floor. You heard it too, didn't you?"

"Yes, I heard it, but you've heard we have a ghost living in our shop, right?"

"I've heard gossip about it, but I didn't believe it. I thought it was just a silly rumor." As he climbed down the ladder he still had a look of bewilderment on his face. I just smiled, reassuring him that it was no rumor. I told Ralph that I had told anyone of the workers to just say the name of Jesus, when they think they have come against this evil spirit.

That experience made a believer of him.

"Stop in the Name of the Law!"

A detective came to retrieve stolen items that had been pawned to us. He was part of the special unit of detectives established by the Jacksonville Sheriff's Office. This unit's main focus was pawn shops because criminals knew they could quickly get rid of their stolen items in the shops.

I was off that day, but Stacy told me what happened.

She led Detective Prescott upstairs. When they reached the top of the stairs, she realized she had forgotten the key to one of the rooms. When she returned with the key, she noticed Detective Prescott had his gun drawn. He had heard movement in one of the rooms.

He had a worried look in his eyes, and the atmosphere had changed. He told her to stay back and headed for the same room where Ralph had heard the noise.

She said, "After he checked all the doors and was satisfied that no one had broken in, he said, "Stacy, I heard someone up here. It felt as if something bumped into me, and the room got cold.'"

Stacy said she smiled and told him, "Detective Prescott, that's Marsha's ghost. You just have to rebuke it in Jesus name, and it will leave." He just looked at her and shook his head and walked down the stairs.

I often wondered why those demonic spirits manifested as they did. To my knowledge not any one ever denied their experienced. Regardless, of what they thought Jesus was always the answer.

Chapter Fifteen

EVERY DOG HAS ITS DAY

I had the day off from the pawn shop. The kids and I had started back attending church. Rick would join us at times. He was still writing Christian songs. Life was fairly normal and it felt good.

My family was growing up. DeAnna was married now. Ricky and Scotty had afterschool jobs at Kentucky Fried Chicken.

A couple weeks earlier I received a phone call from my friend Cherry, who informed me that Jerome, my ex-husband, was back in Jacksonville for a visit. I shared this with Rick. We knew he'd probably want to see Ricky and Scotty. DeAnna was old enough to make her own decision as to whether to see him or not. They hadn't been seen him in years. Ricky was now sixteen and Scotty fifteen.

When we divorce Jerome had asked me not to take him to court for not paying child support. In return, he would leave the kids alone until they turned eighteen.

I said, "If that's what you want, I won't file charges for child support money."

I kept my word and never did.

Most people said I was wrong to let him get away with not paying. Maybe I was, but my mindset was that if I had to force someone to give me something, then I didn't want it. Jerome kept his promise and stayed out of contact with the kids.

I hadn't told Ricky or Scotty that Jerome was in town, yet.

Rick was scheduled to go into the recording studio later that evening with his band.

I was cooking earlier than usual and decided to take a break from making dinner and called DeAnna. I told her Jerome was in town but I had not told the boys. I wanted to let her know first all she said was, "Oh."

While her and I talked. Rick sat in his recliner tuning his guitar while watching television.

I decided to let Erika and Jazz play outside a little longer before calling them in for dinner. I heard the porch door open fast and thought the girls had come home.

I looked up, and there stood a man I initially didn't recognize. Rick immediately jumped to his feet.

"Where's the bathroom?" he asked. When he spoke, I recognized his voice it was Jerome!

I saw the wide-eyed look on Rick's face, wondering why this stranger had just barged into his home.

Surprised I said, "Jerome?" I would not have recognized him in public. He had gained weight and of course was older.

Jerome stumbled toward the bathroom.

Rick followed him but stopped in the hallway. I heard Jerome urinating, and I guess that was enough to keep Rick from pursuing him. I quickly put down the phone I wasn't sure what Rick was going to do.

I told Rick, "He's drunk."

Jerome staggered back to the living room. I had not seen nor heard from this man in over twelve years. Seeing him now seemed surreal. I didn't know what was going to happen next.

Rick seemed way too calm. He stood close to Jerome but didn't say anything.

Jerome had literally invaded our house and was treading on dangerous ground.

He asked, "Got any beer?"

Without waiting for an answer, he headed for the kitchen.

I repeated, "He's drunk."

DeAnna was still on the phone and was hearing everything that was happening. When I picked up the phone again DeAnna asked, "Jerome is in the house with dad?"

She and her brothers thought of Rick as their father because he had been part of their lives since they were young. She couldn't believe her biological father had just walked into our home, unannounced and without permission.

Rick and Jerome had never met each other. I was sure there was no love lost between them.

DeAnna said, "Call me back, Mom," and hung up.

"Hey Jerome," Rick said as Jerome came out of the kitchen.

He asked again, "Got any beer?"

Rick said, "No, we never have beer in our house. Marsha and I don't drink. Hey, the boys aren't here. Why don't you come back when they're here?"

Rick's attitude and demeanor shocked me. I thought, *He's actually handling this situation, very well.*

Jerome headed for the door and Rick followed him. When Jerome reached the door, he turned and pointed his finger right in Rick's face. "Every dog has his day, you'll have yours," he snarled.

Rick jerked his head back. I watched as Rick's face turn white. Before I could blink, Rick punched him in the stomach.

I immediately dialed 911. I told the operator what had happened. She asked for the address and told me the police were on the way.

Jerome fell over Rick's homemade wooden workout bench. He reached down for one of Rick's work out weights to hit him with.

Rick raised his hand, that is when I saw his pocket knife, and it was open. He had stabbed Jerome in the stomach.

I didn't know Rick had even pulled his knife out of his pocket. He went to stab him again.

I grabbed his hand to stop him but caught the blade of his knife and cut my thumb. I screamed, "Don't kill him! Stop! Stop!"

I grabbed Rick around the waist and tried to pull him away from Jerome. My adrenaline was running high. Although my thumb was bleeding, I didn't feel it. I knew I had to control Rick, or he may kill Jerome.

Rick picked up Jerome by his seat of his breaches and threw him out in the yard. Jerome stagger to his truck and drove off. I could hear sirens getting louder and knew the police were near.

This all happened in a matter of minutes. I was traumatized but somehow in control. My concern was Erika and Jazz coming home and experiencing this awful sight.

Three police cars arrived and immediately separated Rick and I. Rick told his story to one policeman while I sat in one of the police cars and told another officer what I had witnessed. The third officer drove off in the direction Jerome had gone. Within minutes, we heard more sirens, but this time it was an ambulance.

Although the officer I was speaking with was nice, he grilled me. I knew his questions were based on his knowledge that I was the ex-wife.

He asked, "When was the last time you saw your ex-husband?"

"About twelve years ago." I replied.

He continued asking the same questions, but in a different way. "How long has it been since your ex-husband contacted his kids?"

I understood why he had to question me. That was his job and what he had been trained to do. I had told him the truth, though.

Finally, I said to him, "Sir, I realize you're doing your job, but my story's not going to change no matter how many times you ask me I'm being truthful. I have no reason to lie or try to hide anything from you."

"Jerome broke into our house. I did know he was in town, but I haven't had any contact with him. Rick tried to lure him out of the house and told him to come back when the boys were home."

His eyes searched my face, and I could tell he was trying to make a decision concerning how to handle this situation.

I asked, "Don't you see enough darkness in the world every day? I can understand it's hard to differentiate between a lie and a truth, but all I want is peace. We tried to make good out of a bad situation. Rick defended himself after being threatened in his own home."

The officer looked up from writing his report. "How did he threaten him?"

"He told him, 'Every dog has its day, and you'll have yours'. He pointed his finger in Ricks face. In fact, his finger almost touched him."

I watched the young policeman's eyes soften. It seemed like he finally believed that I had told him the truth.

He smiled. "Okay, Mrs. Yarbrough. Please wait by my car."

He got out of his car and walked toward the officer talking with Rick. He motioned for the officer to join him.

The other policeman who had taken off looking for Jerome had returned. The three officers huddled together. The one who talked with me walked back over.

"Mrs. Yarbrough, just thought I'd let you know that we found your ex-husband. He's being taken to the hospital now."

I let out a big sigh of relief.

The cop continued, "Some kids told the officer that they saw a man bleeding and going into one of the backyards. They found him collapsed on the back porch. The residents weren't home."

I learned later that the back porch belonged to my friend Cherry and her husband Sammy. Who had told us Jerome was in town, we had all been friends back when we were married.

I watched all three policemen exchange information and discuss what had taken place. I silently prayed and thanked the Lord that His grace was all I needed.

One of the officers in charge approached Rick and handed him the police report. "You need to take this to the state's attorney office and file a criminal trespassing report on Jerome."

I praised the Lord, relieved that this part of this horrible experienced was over.

We both were shaken up but Rick was determined to continue with his recording session. As we drove to the studio I silently thank the Lord. He said He would never leave nor forsake me and He was true to His Word.

Rick was always on a natural high before going in the studio, but his adrenaline tonight was working overtime. I listened as he told what had just happened to his musicians. Everyone was surprised and couldn't believe he didn't cancel the session.

I watched through the studio glass as Rick put every ounce of his energy into the recording. His talent and ability to record after that ordeal proved he was a true musician.

When the recording session ended, and we were driving home, I felt as if I had been in a nightmare. I knew the Lord had worked it to our good, yes it was awful experience but I shuttered to imagine what it may have been.

The next day, Rick woke up with his hand swollen and blue. He went to the emergency room and came home with his hand in a cast. He had several broken bones. It was a miracle he could even play his bass guitar last night.

We found out the Jerome had been taken to the hospital and underwent emergency surgery. He stayed in the hospital several days. Rick and I prayed for him and put him and his family on the prayer list at church.

Standing Guard with a 12-Gauge

About six months after that happened on a Friday night. I received a phone call. "Marsha, Marsha. I'm Jerry's wife!" she cried. I heard the panic in her voice. "He's Jerome's younger brother. Jerome and Jerry are drunk. They have guns and are on their way to your house to kill ya'll."

Of course, I had known Jerome's younger brother Jerry. I had met his wife years earlier but had no contact with them in many years. Now here she was telling me this horrible news.

"Please tell Rick not to kill Jerry. He has nothing to do with this, I tried to stop them, but they're drunk." I was stunned and tried to reassure her that we were going to call the police but she was more panicky than I was.

I told Rick what the call was about. His eyes widened in fear, and his body tensed up he was going into a protective mode. He would kill to protect himself and family. This was something I didn't want to happen.

Fear swept over me, my two girls were home. Ricky and Scotty were spending the night out, so I knew they would be safe. My concerned was for Erika and Jasmine.

I wanted to get them out of this situation as soon as possible.

I called DeAnna and told her what Jerry's wife had said.

She said, "Mom, bring the girls to my house." I quickly packed up the girls' and drove them to DeAnna's.

On my drive back home, I prayed asking the Lord to send His angels for protection not only for us but also for Jerome and Jerry. I prayed in my heavenly language because the spirit of fear was still tormenting me.

By the time I arrived back home. The house was dark, I could see no lights. This gave me a weird feeling. I thought this isn't a good sign for all the lights to be off.

I pulled into the driveway slowly. I got out of the car and cautiously walked up to the front porch door. The dark felt oppressive, and my heart was beating faster than normal. Were Jerome and Jerry inside? What was I about to encounter, I was scared.

I opened the front porch door, then slowly opened the door to a pitch-dark living room. I heard Rick whispering, he was on the phone. I could tell that he was talking with the police. He hung the phone up and shined a flashlight in my face.

"I called the police," he said. "I told them we were being threatened. They said if they came to the house with guns to call them."

"Call them when they come with guns?" I asked I guess I was expecting a different answer. "Why can't they come now?" I asked.

He answered "Because no crime has been committed. That's what they said, but we have the right to protect ourselves if they enter our house."

A knot formed and twisted in my stomach. I wanted to scream but didn't. I wanted to run but didn't. I wanted to wake up from this nightmare.

Rick handed me a twelve-gauge pump shotgun that I had purchased at the pawn shop. He said "Go stand guard by the bedroom window that faces the street. Keep the lights off. I'll stay on the porch and watch with my .357 Smith & Wesson revolver."

The shotgun and I sat in the dark bedroom. I felt like I was stuck in a scene of some gangster movie. How did my life get to this point? I would have never expected that I would be sitting by a window with a 12-gauge shotgun protecting my home.

Each sound I heard launched me into an abnormal, hypersensitive alert mode.

Finally, the light of dawn rose slowly and I watched the darkness of this night give way to a very welcomed morning.

God, once again, had posted His angels to stand guard. No shootout. No deaths. Nothing but fear, and it had proven to be false.

I worshipped and thanked the Lord, He never once failed me.

Chapter Sixteen

CHALLENGES AND MORE

Everyday brought a challenge that left me feeling like an octopus pulled in eight different directions. I wasn't sure which way to go, and I constantly stayed in survival mode. I never let go of Jesus, although I wasn't attending church much. My prayers became more pleading than believing.

I couldn't depend on Rick for any stability especially when it came to helping financial. He was caught up in his music and I found it less stressful to just let him be. His moods were unpredictable changing like the wind.

The boys were in their teens. Ricky hung out with his best friend Tommy. Scotty though hung out with older boys in the neighborhood and often skipped school.

Scotty was arrested with some of these boys for petty crimes, but their crimes escalated. I knew he was headed for trouble. I tried to make him understand that his actions would take him to places he did not want to go. He proved me right, and he was in and out of juvenile detention center.

At fifteen, Scotty was arrested for theft. The judge adjudicated him as an adult because of his juvenile record. He turned sixteen in jail and was sentenced to twelve years in an adult prison. My heart broke for him facing this horrible sentence, but he was man enough to put the blame on himself.

When Ricky turned seventeen, he wanted to join the Navy. But he had one big hurdle to cross, namely that he had missed a lot of school due to his health. He had been diagnosed with heart trouble, asthma, and seizures when he was younger, and this put him back a year.

He would be eighteen in a few months, the age required to enlist in the Navy. We went to the school board to ask them to allow him to drop out of public school and complete his high school in junior college. I was told that I had to get a release request from the supervisor who was the only person who could grant this.

On the first visit, the supervisor was very nice but definitely not in agreement with our request. He had good reason too. He let me know that this was not the first time he had been asked to do this.

He said "Mrs. Yarbrough, most students never finish high school after they quit. Unless you can prove Ricky has a medical condition, he'll have to get his diploma at a public high school."

This was not an option. The Navy would not take him with his health record. We believed God would heal him and that he would pass the Navy physical.

I prayed for both Scotty and Ricky fervently. They both were facing life changes, and I could do nothing to fix either one of them. I felt so helpless and desperate. I could not express my feeling to Rick, either. How do you make anyone understand the fear and pain that a mother's heart feels? He brought more stress on me because he was so critical and condescending.

I had to look and act strong. I still had two young girls at home. I needed to bring as much stability as possible. I had no one but Jesus, and He was such a friend and comfort to me.

Before Scotty was sentenced, I made many trips to the Public Defender's office trying to keep up with his case. They had moved him from the city jail to a different facility nicknamed the Pea Farm. Back in the day, the prisoners worked in the fields, and that's how it got the nickname.

It was about a forty-minute ride from my house. Visiting hours were twice a week, from six to eight p.m. I brought him his Bible and reassured him that somehow Jesus would work this out for his good.

My heart broke for Scotty. We lived in a neighborhood that was considered inner city and he wanted to fit in. Scotty really was a timid child. He was not one to spend the night away from home. He was a true momma's boy. The real Scotty was tenderhearted and smart, but in some way, I felt like he wanted Rick's approval, not that Rick had ever condoned what Scotty was doing. But Scotty saw Rick as being tough when he was a teenager. Maybe he thought this would impress Rick or his peers.

Scotty received his high school diploma while incarcerated and made exceptionally high grades. In all of the uncertainty he faced at his age, he held himself together in front of me, not arrogant but humble. He didn't allow me to see his fear. I knew he was scared and rightly so, but he always put a brave face on for me. Scotty's outlook was mom you know I will be fine. You know it will all work out for my good, he was challenging my faith. I realized that my words or Gods words stood in the middle of his storm. He turned sixteen while he was waiting for sentencing. All I could give him was a birthday card.

I was still determined to help Ricky with his goal of getting into the Navy. On my day off, I would go to the supervisor's office, pleading with him to allow Ricky to leave public school so he could earn his high school diploma early, he only had a few months until his eighteenth birthday.

I remembered a story in the Bible about a lady who continuously asked the judge for justice. Finally, the judge told the woman that she had worn him out and that he would grant her request. I reminded the Lord that I had prayed continuously for Him to change the heart of the supervisor. He had changed that judge's heart. So, I believed He could also change the supervisor heart too.

Each time I went to the supervisor's office, I always said the same thing. "I completely understand your position, but I can guarantee you that Ricky will complete his high school and join the Navy."

On my fourth trip, I waited patiently to see him again. I felt like we had become somewhat friends, he recognized me by sight now.

His secretary opened his door and with a smile and ushered me to his office. He greeted me as he always did, but this time, he handed me the papers for Ricky to go to junior college.

I thanked him and shook his hand, telling him this was an answer to my prayers. Ricky not only earned his diploma early but with a high GPA while also working a part-time job. I sent the supervisor a letter to thank him letting him know what Ricky had accomplished, and he was now in boot camp. When the day came for him to leave I wanted it to be a good one.

But it turned out to be very hectic. When we went to the Navy's recruitment office, his recruiter said there had been a discrepancy in his diploma, and we needed to have it corrected. The college said he had not earned enough credits to receive his high school diploma, so we had to get that straighten out.

Finally, they realized their mistake. We hurried back to the recruitment office with the corrected paper. Ricky had a flight to catch, and we were racing against time. He needed some tennis shoes, and I had very little money, so we rushed to a Family Dollar trying to find the cheapest shoes we could buy. I barely had enough money to purchase them. I felt so bad because he should have had a party the night before and nice shoes like most of the young men leaving home for the first time.

Ricky never once complained, though. He was only allowed to take a pair of shoes, underwear, and the clothes he was wearing. He had all these in a brown paper bag.

I watched him as he walked down the corridor toward the plane and wave goodbye. I cried on the way home.

Both my boys were now gone. One had gone up to the Great Lakes for boot camp, and the other down south to prison.

Both boys left in the same month, the house felt so different. When I opened the door to the boys' room, tears rolled down my cheeks as I saw both of their empty beds. This was the first time they had been away and I knew they weren't returning any time soon, either. Thank God for Erika and Jazz, I was not used to not having my kids around.

This would be an emotional time for any mother, but to me, it was super rough.

Rick put another band together and was still writing and recording songs in the studio. He was satisfied with his life, but I wasn't with mine. He was still irrational at times, and I was tired of trying to make things right. He only worked long enough to pay for studio time. I found every day exhausting, and I struggled within myself not to get bitter. Nothing had changed, except for me. Deep inside, I wanted change. I would read my Bible and constantly prayed and asked the Lord for wisdom.

Moving Right Along and Along

My mother lived in Pembroke Pines, Florida, in the Fort Lauderdale area. I felt a strong urge to leave Rick. However, I needed a plan set in place before making any move.

First, I had to find a job. This thought came to me, I could clean houses. I had never considered this before.

I called Mary, my friend in Miami. Who was the lady who had witnessed my "trip" years earlier? I told her my plan.

She said, "Marsha, your timing is right on. I have a friend who cleans houses and is leaving her business. We can go into business together. I'll call her and ask her for advice on how to begin."

After talking with her, I got a peaceful feeling.

I was still working at the pawn shop and needed to let my boss know my plan. I told him I could not give him an exact date when I would leave. He reassured me that would not be a problem and that I could work until I had things in order.

I didn't mention this to anyone especially Rick. I knew I had to plan this out ahead of time. I didn't want to hurt Rick, but it was now a matter of survival for me and the girls.

Rick got offered a three-day job on a training film for the Georgia Highway Patrol. He had worked with them before and enjoyed it. They used people to recreate scenarios in a patrolman's life.

Rick said he was acting and I guess he was. He told me what day he was going to Georgia. Now I would schedule my get away.

That day finally came. That morning, after Rick left for Georgia, I took the kids to school. I then came home to get ready for our trip. After packing our clothes, I picked out some of the girl's favorite toys and other things they would want to bring. I sat down and wrote Rick a letter. This wasn't his first letter I had written hoping that he would understand I was pleading for our marriage. I hoped my words would change him, but they never did.

This time was different, though. I was leaving with a clear plan not out of fear.

I looked around, recalling all of the fond memories of my childhood home. My recollections of raising my children in this house came with mixed emotions. We'd had some good times as a family in this house but I had to move ahead now. Things would never be the same again.

I wasn't sure what I was feeling. I loaded up my little 1985 Plymouth Champ and drove to the school to pick up the girls.

I walked into the school's office and one of the school's secretary asked if she could help me. I said, "I'm taking my girls out of school and moving to Miami."

She looked over the rim of her glasses. "Okay. You'll need to fill out the withdrawal papers."

After I the completed papers and gave them back to her, she called both girls' names over the intercom and told them to come to the office with all of their books. I waited, trying not to pace as I wondered what the girls must be thinking.

It took a few moments before they both came. Surprised was written on both of their faces when they saw me.

Erika asked, "Mom why are you here?"

Jazz added, "Yeah, Mom, what's wrong?"

"Nothing's wrong. We're going on a trip."

The clerk knitted her eyebrows together, obviously puzzled that the girls had not known they were being withdrawn from school. She handed me copies of the withdrawal papers still with her puzzled look.

I thanked her and smiled. The girls were still asking me what was going on. Seeing some of their stuffed animals in the backseat stoked their curiosity even more.

"We're going on a journey," I said, forcing a smile.

They both said. "Where are we going?"

"It's a secret."

"What? Why it is a secret?"

"Are you kidding, Mom?"

"Did you really withdraw us from school?"

I was still forcing a smile. I didn't want to discuss anything at this time. I had to do what I felt was right. I kept my secret as we drove towards I-95 south.

After we passed Saint Augustine, I said, "Guess what? We're moving to Miami."

"Mom," both said in unison. It was not a good response. I could hear the "oh no" in their voices. I had prepared myself, but I had not prepared them. I had not given them time to process it. I hadn't even given them a chance to say goodbye to their friends or even taken the time to pack what they wanted. I understood why they weren't happy.

"Why? We don't want to move."

My smile faded.

"I know, girls, but I had to make a hard decision for us. I think it's the right one."

I knew they understood my reason, because they too, had experienced the chaos in our house.

I tried to reassure them. "Hey, it's a new beginning. You'll love Miami. Well, actually, we're going to Fort Lauderdale, right on the county line."

This too was going to be a surprise for my mother. I had not told her either but knowing my mother, it wouldn't be a problem. My father died in 1972 and my mother's sister died in 1976. My mother and her brother in law Woodrow married in 1979 with all of the family's blessings. So, my uncle became my step-dad, and my cousins became my step-brothers. We were one big happy family.

Woodrow and Mom were very happy and enjoyed their golden years together.

When I arrived at my mom's house, the kids and I went straight through the garage that led to the kitchen. Mom was washing dishes and had her back to the door.

When she turned around, her head jerked back in surprise as a big smile brighten her face. After we all hugged and kissed, I sent the kids out to unpack the car. They had a large house, so the kids took the large guest bedroom.

When we were alone, Mom stared at me with a raised eyebrow.

"Mom, I had to leave and start afresh."

"I understand," she said and hugged me.

I knew she had worried about my situation with Rick. She had never put Rick down but often asked if Rick was working. I always reassured her that his music career would soon be supporting us.

My mom was one special lady. After we settled in, I enrolled the girls in their new school.

Mary and I started our cleaning service. We called it M&M Cleaning Services. We started out with six accounts that Mary friend gave us. We grew it into one hundred accounts in a matter of months.

Most of our business was cleaning condos. In addition, I worked two part-time jobs. I worked nights at K-Mart as well as for a catering service when needed. The catering service did mostly Jewish Bar Mitzvahs. I saved enough money and moved us into a two-bedroom house in the same neighborhood.

We attended a spirit-filled church in Miami. Although I worked a lot more, because the cost of living was higher but I was peaceful.

In the letter I left Rick I told him where I was going, I knew it was the right thing to do. Weekly he would call my mom's house to check on us.

I would return his call letting him know that girls were safe and happy. I never gave him our address though. We were cordial to each other. However, I did have to admit I missed some of those good times we had, but I would always remind myself they were only temporary.

This Can't Be

Coming home from work I thought, *This can't be.*

Rick's blue van was parked in my driveway. My heart raced, and my stomach churned. I forced myself to calm down before walking inside.

There he was, sitting on the couch with the girls. His blue-green eyes lit up when he saw me.

He stood up and embraced me as if seven months of not seeing each other had never happened. Admittedly, his strong arms embracing me felt natural.

"How did you find me, Rick?" I asked.

"You told me you lived close to your mom, so I drove to your mom's and then around the neighborhood. When I saw the school bus, I followed it until I saw the girls get off.

He had driven over three hundred miles to find us. We talked, and again he said all those things I had heard many times before.

This was the longest we had ever been separated, so I told him he could stay, but he would have to find a job. He wanted to prove to us he wanted his family.

After three weeks, he still had not found a job. I wasn't sure if he was really trying. I left work early one day just to see if what I was feeling was true.

Sure enough, his van was parked in the driveway. I was mad. All those negative feelings and fear rose up inside me. I hated what I was feeling it triggered bad memories and I was angry that I had allowed myself to get back in the same situation I had tried to escape from.

I opened the front door and had my speech ready to go but before I could say anything, he gave me a hug and smiled. "Marsha, I got a job doing maintenance at Joe Robbie's stadium."

My firm look turned into a smile. But after a month, he got laid off or at least that what he said. It seemed we were destined to return to Jacksonville. The girls wanted to return to their old neighborhood and school, I was outvoted.

We came back to our Drayton Street house, and life started all over again. The girls were happy being back in their old neighborhood. I hoped this separation had changed him. Sadly, I allowed myself to believe a lie. I did away with any thought of living a healthy life with Rick.

I knew I had returned to the hell I tried so hard escape from. Church was my refuge. I refused to miss church and insisted the girls come too. I looked forward to Sundays that was my only peace. I could leave all my cares behind. The bible said that Jesus inhabited the praise of His people. I knew that all I could do was praise Jesus. I worshipped with my hands lifted to my Savior.

I believed that in due time, God would have His way in my life. I replaced my previous prayers from "I need this, Lord" and "Please change Rick" to "Change me. Lord, change me!"

The Holy Spirit did His work. The Bible became my best friend. I would fall asleep while meditating on what I read.

I didn't understand some stories in the Bible, especially those in the Old Testament, but I read them anyway. I studied the notes I made at church and researched each scripture.

The Holy Spirit was teaching me. He had me in His school. I was changing, although my external circumstances were not. I still had chaos and strife, but as I changed, the fear, the doubt, and all the negativity did not affect me as it once did. I was coming out of a woe-is-me pity party.

The Lord spoke to me one time in very simple language. "You're not God, and you can't change anyone. That's not your responsibility. You are only responsible for allowing the Holy Spirit to impart His Life to you."

So, I released myself from trying to make Rick into what I thought he should be. I learned a very valuable lesson that you can't change people. You can impart wisdom, and encouragement, but change can only take place when it is embraced. You need to love them where they're at, even though you don't like or agree with their actions.

I found myself being very judgmental not so much of others but especially me. It seems I was failing at trying to be like Jesus. I had to apologize to the Lord so many times a day. But the Holy Spirit would graciously remind me of Jesus great love for me, my heart would come alive to His Love.

Chapter Seventeen

"YOU NEED TO DIVORCE ME"

Rick took a night-time job with a security company. But I knew him and his pattern never changed it was for him to get enough money to go back into the studio to do more songs.

But it still was a blessing to me. First, he was working, and second, I had some time to myself.

I continued to immerse myself in the Bible and prayer. I'd learned to trust the Lord at a different level than I had previously. I prayed more than ever in my prayer language, and I could sense the Holy Spirit leading me.

I continued to ask the Lord to change me. He was teaching me not to lean on my own understanding and try to figure out what God would do next.

I desired change and I craved correction in my life. Real change only comes from within, and I wanted to change deep inside me.

I wanted the Holy Spirit to have His way in me. This was not an easy thing for me to ask.

My mind was full of fear, doubts, worry, anger, and disappointments. It stayed in survival mode. Now I had to believe that the Lord's word was true. I had to practice the scripture that said in II Corinthians 10:5 "Cast down all imaginations and every high thing that exalts itself against the knowledge of God."

So, I continually battled for God's Word to rise up in my mind and eradicate all my fears.

Romans 8:28 tells us that "… all things work for the good …."

I must have quoted that ten thousand times a day, during the constant battle that took place within me. Regardless of what life handed me.

Change isn't easy, especially when it's genuine and comes from the Lord; it goes against human nature. When the Bible speaks of the old man dying, putting that old nature to death is very painful. I was so used to justifying my thoughts.

In II Corinthians 5:17, it said that when we accept Jesus as Lord we are born again and that old things are passed away and become new. I had gone through five child births. But this born again in the Spirit was different. Besides, you could ask for drugs to get you through it. I had no drugs to get me through this. My mind would battle against God's Word. I found it more comforting to believe in what I was experiencing than to have faith that it would change. I often told God He was not helping me either. From where I sat, I couldn't see how this was for my good. The Holy Spirit was patient with me and reminds me that His ways were higher than mine. I told him to give me wings so I could fly to those higher places.

Donuts Anyone?

One Sunday morning, the girls and I were getting ready for church. Rick had stopped on his way home from his job and bought some donuts. This was a rare treat, and the girls were more than eager to enjoy this surprise. I could hear them in the dining room moving about while I finished getting ready

"Marsha, you want a donut?" Rick yelled from the kitchen.

"Did you buy a Coke too?" I yelled back. For some reason, I have always liked Coke with donuts. I'm not much of a donut eater, but whenever I eat them, I always wash them down with a Coke.

"No, I didn't," he yelled back.

"Never mind, I'll pass." I answered.

I continued brushing my hair, not even thinking about what I had said to Rick. I overheard Rick say to the girls, "Your mom thinks she's too good to eat donuts."

I didn't like the tone of his voice.

I finished applying my lipstick, and Rick came into the bathroom. He stood in the doorway his bulky frame took up three-fourths of the small door.

He asked, "You think you're too good to eat donuts without a Coke?"

I answered "No, of course not."

I watched his eyes turn dark. That was not a good sign. He turned and headed back to the kitchen.

I called Erika. "Get my purse, and you and Jasmine go on to the car. I'll be out in a minute."

A couple minutes later, I heard the front door close and knew the girls were out of the house. I quickly finished getting ready. Rick began cursing at me from the living room. I knew trying to resolve this stupid argument would be in vain.

I turned to find Rick blocking the bathroom door again. He was mad, dangerously mad, and he still cussed at me.

I didn't want to get trapped in this tiny space with him. "I'm sorry, Rick."

He told me how ungrateful I was. My concern was not letting him corner me in the bathroom.

This wasn't the first time I had seen his eyes turn a yellowish color. This was not Rick, but a demonic spirit. This spirit wanted to kill me.

I had a flashback to the time when Jasmine was a baby, and I was holding her. He had gotten mad at me and shot at me with a .22-caliber pistol. Of course, he missed, but it put a small hole in the dining room wall.

He told me he just wanted to scare me, not kill me. This spirit would periodically take control of him, and from my point of view, it had him this morning.

This had nothing to do with me not wanting a donut. I wondered if something bad had happened to him at work. I never knew what could set off this spirit.

I said, "Rick, I just want to go to church. The girls are waiting."

Then that spirit spoke. "Marsha, you had better divorce me before I kill you." Then he walked away.

I let out a sigh of relief that this ended with nothing more than words.

I recognized that spirit speaking and knew that Satan wanted me dead. I had always known that spirit wanted me dead.

I kept quiet in the car and turned my Christian radio station louder as we drove to church. I immersed myself in worship, allowing His presence to flow through me. How I loved Him. He, the Creator of the universe, cared for me.

I glanced around at the people worshipping Jesus. Some of them had their eyes closed while others worshipped with their hands and faces lifted toward heaven. It didn't matter to me how they worshipped because I was worshipping with them.

Lifting my hands in sweet surrender to my Savior, I felt hot tears flowing down my cheeks. I let them stay there without wiping them off.

The ministry of the Word was rich. I took notes, wanting to remember as much as I could. I wondered if anyone else had their life threatened this morning.

Erika hadn't gone to her class and was busy writing on my notepad. Toward the end of the service, I wrote Erika a note.

I asked, "What should I do with Dad?"

She wrote back, "Divorce him."

What I meant to write was, "Should we bring Dad back something to eat after church?" This had been our Sunday routine and usually it was a chicken dinner from a fast food place.

I'm not sure whether I intentionally left that out of my note, but she gave me my answer. Was this the Holy Spirit speaking?

I did bring him something to eat, but he was asleep by the time we got home, which was a relief. I had received my answer from the Lord. Now I had to wait on His timing.

Obeying His Voice

The weeks went by as if everything was fine. Rick didn't realize that somewhere along the way, I had left him, not physically but emotionally. I was completely released from Rick, although I still lived with him. I no longer felt a connection to him. Rick never noticed I had detached myself. I was going through the motions of being his wife. This proved to me that he was not in tune with my emotions, sad.

I thought of other marriages and wondered if they really stayed together out of love or security.

My mind went back to the beginning of our relationship and the closeness we once had. For years I believed in him. What held him back and haunted him was not lack of talent, but his own demons. He had embraced his demons while I fought them.

I had to allow myself to face the truth that everything and everyone changes. I had prayed for the Lord to change him but soon realized some people just refuse to change. This was painful, because I felt deceived. I prayed for the Holy Spirit to change me, regardless of what it would cost me.

I knew Rick believed in Jesus and the Lord wanted to use him. I couldn't understand why he refused to trust the Lord totally. Eventually, the Holy Spirit let me understand that Rick's refusal to give up complete control was out of fear, not out of rebellion. The

Lord showed me that fear was one of Satan greatest weapons. Fear of not pleasing God, fear of not being worthy enough, fear of being judged and always messing up. It grieves God when His children think He is a God of judgment and not mercy and love.

Rick and I had another terrible argument, and the Holy Spirit spoke very clearly to me. "There is a spirit of murder here, and you need to leave."

I called my childhood friend Brenda, who had recently gone through a divorce and was living across town. Rick would never look for us there.

Brenda was more than glad to have us stay with her and her younger daughter Tiffany. This time I told the girls what I had planned but assured them that this was going to be a short stay. Again, we packed our clothes and headed to Brenda's.

I contacted a paralegal, knowing this was the least expensive way to obtain a divorce. I was asking for nothing in the divorce, I knew he would not contest anything.

The house was in my name. My father had built it, and I was raised there, but at this time, I just wanted peace and safety. I allowed Rick to stay there for the time being. All Rick had was his guitars and an old Ford van. He wasn't working again, so there was no need to ask him to pay child support.

I filed the divorce papers through a paralegal. Within nine weeks, I stood before a judge who granted my divorce. I phoned Rick to let him know we were divorced.

He said, "Someone stuck an envelope with the divorce papers through the broken jalousie window in the front porch door, but I tore them up."

He then proceeded to cuss me out over the phone. "We're not divorced because I didn't sign those papers," he protested.

"Regardless of whether you signed them or not, Rick, we are divorced. I'll give you a month to pack up your things and be out of my house."

He slammed down the phone.

I was no longer dominated by that spirit. I was free. This was a big change for me, but I was happy.

I wasn't trying to hurt him. However, I was angry at him for not fighting harder and allowing God to change him.

I continuously sought the Lord. I purposely reminded myself that Jesus would never leave me. Jesus had promised me a good future and I was going forward.

Divorce was freedom to me, not frightening. Some women are afraid of being alone or not having a man to take care of them. Those things were the least of my concerns.

Chapter Eighteen

MURDER AND THE BLOOD

It was time for us to move back to our house. I thanked Brenda for taking us in and giving us a place of refuge, she was my oldest friend. We had grown up together and were like sisters.

Rick left within the month and we moved back. I wasn't happy to be living there again, though. I didn't have a choice. At least I didn't have to pay rent. My high electric bill made up for it, though, the house was old.

It wasn't unusual to see the police patrolling our neighborhood three to four times a day. Drugs and drug dealers had moved in to what had once been a safe family neighborhood.

The pawn shops were experiencing the same thing with increased crime. The clientele had changed. My boss saw the writing on the wall and decided to sell.

A longtime friend of mine wanted to buy the shop and asked me to go in with him. He would bring the money, and I would bring the expertise to run it. I was excited with this new venture. I had dreams of being financially stable and moving us to a better place. My dreams of financial stability came to an end. I couldn't even take a paycheck

I was barely hanging on at home or at work. I was in a dark hole and scarcely could see the sunlight. Everything was falling apart the more I tried the worse it got. I was mentally and physically tired, disgusted and broke.

To top it off, my car engine blew up, and now I had no transportation. I had to ride the bus to work. At times I would walk home just to clear my head it was only about three miles.

The girls were adjusting to their newfound freedom. Since their dad had always been home, at least I didn't have to worry about leaving them alone.

Erika was fourteen and Jazz was twelve. I had strict rules for them to follow. When I was at work, only two friends were allowed at the house, but I knew my rules weren't always kept. They were not to go outside of the yard.

Erika wanted her freedom as most teens, so she decided she ought to be able to do like her friends. I told her that was not happening so we did have our disagreements to put it mildly. Jazz was caught in the middle of the turmoil. She did really well, considering she was the youngest and Erika often bullied her.

So now I had no car, no money, and the fear of raising two pretty girls in a drug infested neighborhood. I was scarcely bringing food in the house. Plus, Rick stalked me. Before he moved out, he had cut a large hole in the floor of one of the bedroom closets. He covered it will a piece of carpet, I would have never noticed it, but the girls showed it to me.

I called the police to report it, if anything happened to me, there would be a documented report. He had placed a piece of a cardboard box under the house, and it looked as if he had slept there and had access to my house anytime he wanted.

The officer said, "This is not good for your ex-husband to be living under your house, it could be become very dangerous for you." I agreed.

I nailed up that part of the floor as best as I could and put a padlock on the outside of the closet door trying to secure it but I still did not feel safe.

I told my business partner I was sorry, but I needed to give up my partnership. I just couldn't continue and doing so wasn't fair to him either. He was very understanding.

My electricity and water were turned off for nonpayment. DeAnna asked if her and Mike could keep the girls with them, until I could get back on my feet. They lived at the beach and I knew the girls would be better off there than in our neighborhood. I hated to be without them but I knew at this time it was the best for them, not for me, though.

I cried out to the Lord again, questioning and accusing Him of not caring what was happening to me and my family. Then I would apologize and tell Him it wasn't Him I was mad at. Than quote His word back to Him. "All things work together for good." Inwardly I was really challenging Him and of course He knew it.

Kill, Steal, and Destroy

After the girls left to stay with DeAnna, I was alone in a dark house without electricity and water. At night, I went out and turned on the water with a wrench so that I could take a bath and flush the toilet.

I had bought a .38 revolver from the pawn shop. One night as I as was lying on the couch and listening to a Christian radio station.

A spirit of suicide came on me. It wasn't what I had expected, either. It was very settled, not scary or emotional, just a matter-of-fact feeling. I knew my girls would be taken care of, and I had no regrets about ending my life.

My loaded gun lay on the mantle. I had one flashlight and a battery-operated radio.

When I walked over to get my gun, a thought popped in my head, *"Go and get a Coke and some Red Hot candies from the convenience store first."*

I had borrowed a car from my partner from the pawn shop, for the weekend. So, I drove to the store. The feeling of the night air as I drove with the window down made we want to live. I felt like Hope had walked in, and the scripture that He works all things out for your good came to me. I knew Satan was a liar and God's word was truth.

And just like that, that spirit left me. I'm sure the Holy Spirit convinced me to get the candies and coke.

The next day I felt as if a heavy oppression had lifted off me. I knew I needed a job and fast. I called my mother and asked if she could loan me the money to buy a car. She did, and I found a used car for five hundred dollars. I stayed with my son Ricky and his wife Denise for a while until I could find a job and save enough money to have my utilities turned back on.

I called my friend Dolly, who owned a pawn shop.

I asked "Do you need help?"

"No, but rumor has it your ex-boss is reopening his shop on the other side of town. Give him a call."

I followed her suggestion and called him.

The minute he heard my voice, he said, "Marsha, I've been trying to get a hold of you. Will you come back to work for me?"

My heart leaped with joy. Without hesitation, I said, "Yes."

I had worked with him for over eleven years, and we maintained a good relationship. Now I had the opportunity to again work at a business I knew and really enjoyed. All I could say was Lord thank you, thank you, thank you! I was so humbled that He would open this door for me again. My boss had a partner a man name Stu. Stu didn't know much about the pawn business but was eager to learn. I really enjoyed working with Stu he was an honest good family man.

Rick and I had been divorced for two years. I never stopped him from seeing the girls. We had many conversations during those two years, and we still possessed a very unusual bond. This was hard to explain, especially to someone else. In fact, I could barely comprehend our relationship myself.

Both of us decided to try make a go of it again. The first months were good, but then as time passed, it reverted back to the usual.

On a Wednesday morning, as I getting ready for work, Rick told me he wanted to use my car. I thought this was unusual. He had his van and had never asked to use my car. I didn't question him, though, because I didn't want it to result in an early morning argument.

I was a little annoyed. My morning drive was my time with the Lord, my time alone with Jesus. I always prayed every day for my children. I spoke it out loud too. It wasn't really a prayer but more of a declaration for them: "I apply the blood of the Jesus over DeAnna, Ricky, Scotty, Erika and Jasmine."

Applying the blood of Jesus was a symbolic action that the Lord commandment the Israelites to do when the Angel of death came to destroy the firstborn sons, which represented the saving power of the blood, which is the familiar story of Moses leading the Israelites out of Egypt.

Moses had gone to Pharaoh and told him that God said, "Let my people go."

Each time Pharaoh refused, God sent a plague. The last plague was the angel of death. God commanded the Israelites to take a young lamb without spot or blemish into their house for three days.

On the third day, they sacrificed the lamb and took its blood and sprinkled it over the door. When the death angel came by and saw the blood of the lamb, he passed over their house.

This also represented what Jesus did on the cross for us. He shed His blood so that we could have eternal life and so that death couldn't touch us. Jesus was called the Lamb of God.

I read several books on applying the blood of Jesus. One of those books told a true story of a family living in Germany during World War II, when the air-raid sirens sounded and the bombs fell. The father, a Christian, prayed and asked the Lord to apply His blood over his family. As a result, no one in his family was hurt. They lost their home, but not their lives. So, I did this daily for my children.

I was upset having to give up my time with the Lord. I really cherished my time alone with the Lord.

I never asked Rick why he wanted to use my car. I just climbed into the passenger seat and kept my mouth shut.

Rick drove through the morning traffic on I-95, which was always congested. He started praying out loud and began to apply the blood of Jesus over the family. Although I knew he was sincere, but I couldn't help but wonder how God could be listening to him while simultaneously cussing at traffic and praying too.

He applied the blood over me as we exited the interstate.

I wanted to say, "God's not listening to you because you just cussed everyone out," but I didn't.

He kissed me goodbye. I then reminded him that I would be going to Wednesday night prayer service with my friend after work. Since he had my car, she would bring me home.

Evil, Evil, and Evil

I was surprised to see Stu at work since he was scheduled to be off. We were busy all day long, which was a good day for both of us.

We were almost at the end of the workday, so Stu and I began the routine of closing the store. I started vacuuming the adjacent room while Stu begin to pull out our guns in the showcases. It was a regular routine to lock our guns and jewelry in the large safe each night.

A young teenage girl and an older gentleman came in as we prepared to close. Her yellow headband held back her shoulder-length, curly brown hair and matched her yellow shorts. He wore a green golf shirt with Dockers golf pants with tennis shoes. My first impression was that he was her older brother

They said they only wanted to browse, so I went back to the vacuuming.

I glanced out the window and saw a car with three male occupants pull up in front of the shop. One of the men stepped out with a small towel covering something in his hand and headed to our front door.

I heard in my spirit, "You're about to be robbed."

I ignored that thought and turned the vacuum cleaner off. Of course, whenever you work in an environment like ours, robbery was always a consideration.

I was walking towards the door as the man entered. As soon as he stepped two feet inside the shop, he dropped the towel in his hand, revealing his chrome .380 mm pistol.

He shouted, "Die Mother F*****, die!"

He stood about six feet away from me. The next thing I saw was a flash coming out of the barrel of the pistol.

Everything became surreal, yet my survival mode kicked in, and I immediately sought refuge behind one of our two-foot-tall stereo speakers.

The door opened, and the other two men rushed in. I heard the voice of the man who was with the girl saying, "Please don't hurt us." I could hear the young girl screaming and crying.

Stu had been shot. I knew he was dead. Time seemed to stand still.

I heard glass breaking and knew they were smashing our showcases.

It was as if a ping pong ball was bouncing out of control in my mind. Fear had taken my thoughts captive and I was at the mercy of these killers. I dared not move from my hiding place.

The shooter quickly ran past me and kicked open a vacant office door. That's when he turned around and spotted me. He approached me with, his gun pointed directly at me. He cursed and said he was going to kill me.

He pulled me up by my arm and put the gun against my forehead. "Did you pull any alarms?"

"No," I whimpered. He stuck the gun to the back of my head and pulled me down toward the floor by my hair.

I was bent over, and all I could see was our carpet. I knew he didn't want me to see his face.

My long hair became his leash as he continued to use it to pull me to the other side of the shop. I couldn't see anyone, but I heard all the commotion, and I felt the evil in the air. The young girl was screaming and crying, and the man continued pleading, "Don't kill us."

He let go of my hair and slammed his pistol into my forehead with such force that it made my body go rigid and the force of the blow stood me start up. When that happened, I heard the most powerful voice say with absolute authority, "The blood, the blood."

Those words sounded as if they were directly above my head. The blow from the gun knocked me senseless, but I could still feel him dragging me by my hair.

He pulled me to the front of our pawn counter, right next to the young girl who was lying on the floor. I reached my hand out to touch her and began praying for her. She was terrified, and rightly so. I was face-down on the carpet and the shooter stood over me. He started pistol whipping me on the back of my head. I thought he was going to beat me to death, I continued praying. The thought crossed my mind if I was going to heaven, then I would arrive praying.

I prayed louder in my spirit. The shooter yelled at me to shut up. It's strange, but one of my thoughts was, *this man is not nice, and I wanted him to quit hitting me because it hurts.*

He continued to pistol whip me, though. They used masking tape to cover everyone's eyes, even Stu's, but they didn't tape mine.

I kept going in and out of consciousness. I don't know how long I lay there.

The bell on the front door jiggled, and one of the robbers said, "Let's get out of here."

It was like I was trying to wake up from a nightmare. Somehow, I managed to get off the floor to call the police. I am not sure how long this took me.

I stepped out of the shop, knowing I couldn't go back in there. Stu, my friend, was dead.

Within minutes, police, firemen, and ambulances surrounded our shop. Thank God neither the older man nor the girl was hurt.

The news crews arrived, as well as the usual onlookers. The scene became chaotic with those who needed to be there and those who just came out of curiosity.

I wasn't aware of time. Strangers were trying to be helpful asking me if I was ok. Of course, they too wanted to know what happened.

My friend, who arrived to pick me up for church, pushed her way through the crowd and hugged me. "What happened, Marsha?"

All I could say was "They killed Stu."

I tried to process what had happened, I thought I was in a nightmare and wanted to wake up. My other boss and his wife arrived, and she started crying.

The police roped everything off with the yellow crime tape.

The young girl and the man who had been in the shop stood in our parking lot. I watched the young girl cry as the man comforted her. It was so surreal watching all of this.

Mugshots and X-Rays

Two uniformed policemen pushed their way through the crowd and asked me to come with them. My friend walked with me. Once we were away from the crowd, two other men in suits introduced themselves as detectives.

They asked me if I wanted medical attention, and I told them that I was okay. I didn't want to go to the hospital in an ambulance. A medic came and asked me the same question. I was walking and talking so I thought I was fine just shook up.

One of the detectives said, "Well, we want you to ride with us to the police station."

I hugged my friend and got into the backseat of their dark sedan. I felt numb and desperately wanted to wake up from this nightmare.

As we drove toward downtown, I watched the cars go by and wondered if those people knew that Stu just got murdered. I wanted to cry, but I couldn't.

We entered the police station from the underground parking lot. I felt weak, and one of the detectives held me gently by my arm.

They walked me into a room with tables, chairs, and bookcases that lined the back and side walls.

The older detective said, "Mrs. Yarbrough, the reason we wanted you to come downtown was to look through the mug shots to see if you could pick out anyone involved in your friend's murder. It has been proven that after a trauma like the one you just endured, the mind can recall faces or similar things that could be very helpful within the first couple of hours."

He then set one of the large binders on the table in front of me with hundreds of pictures in it. I looked at several pages of mug shots, but I couldn't focus. I was still in a daze. I became dizzy and nauseous. My right hand hurt, and my palm was turning blue and black.

I said, "I don't feel good. I want to go home."

They both looked at each other in concern. "We're going to take you to the hospital instead."

When I stood up, the room spun, so I sat back down. The detective brought me a drink of water, but I couldn't drink it. I stood up again, and again, I had to sit back down. The nausea had gotten worse.

The younger detective gently helped me up, and the other one steadied me as we as walked back down the hall. Each one had held me, gently placing their hands under my arms.

I sat in the backseat of their car, feeling sick and confused. I heard the detective on their car's dispatch radio, letting the hospital know they were bringing in a robbery victim.

We pulled up at the emergency room doors, and a nurse met us with a wheelchair. They lifted me from the car and set me in it.

They wheeled me directly to triage. To my surprise, I saw Rick, Erika, and Erika's boyfriend John.

When Rick saw me, he rushed over to me. The older detective looked him up and down with a furrowed brow. "Mrs. Yarbrough, do you know this man?"

"Yeah," I managed to mutter, "He's my husband."

One of the detectives stopped him before he reached me. He talked briefly to Rick, before allowing him to pass.

Rick leaned over and kissed me. I could tell he was holding himself together, not wanting to make a scene, especially in front of the detectives.

Rick said, "I'm glad you're alive." A nurse took me back to the emergency room, where she helped me undress and onto the bed. I felt my adrenaline slowly returning. A few minutes later, an orderly wheeled me to radiology. They X-rayed my head and hand.

After what seemed like hours, the doctor came in. "Mrs. Yarbrough, you have a severe concussion plus your hand is broken. I'm admitting you overnight in the hospital for observation."

"No, I want to go home."

I wanted my Bible and I wanted to be in a familiar place and sleep in my own bed.

He insisted that I stay.

"I just want to go home. I understand your concern, Doctor, but I'll be able to rest better at home. All you're going to do is observe me anyway." I was on the verge of screaming.

"Listen, I just witnessed my boss getting murdered. I need to be in a familiar place to feel safe and be with my family."

"I understand you've just experienced a trauma, Mrs. Yarbrough, but promise me you'll come back if you start to feel worse. I need to have a word with your husband."

He stepped out and a few moments later, he returned with Rick. He told Rick that he advised me that I needed to stay overnight but I had refused.

Rick asked, "What do you want to do, Marsha?"

"Go home. I want to go home!"

The doctor said, "Okay, Mrs. Yarbrough. In that case, you'll need to come back in the morning. Mr. Yarbrough, you're going to have to wake her up every few hours. If you can't wake her up, bring her back here immediately." He made me sign a form saying I was leaving Against Medical Advice.

When I walked into my house, I wanted to cry and release every emotion I had bottled up inside me. Strangely, I remained calm. I'm sure some would say I was in shock, but I wasn't sure what I felt.

I had no anger either. I had just come face to face with the evillest of spirits, and it had touched my life yet in spite of that, I felt a deep sense of peace. A peace I could not produce within myself. I also had this overwhelming feeling of forgiveness for those robbers and the murderer.

How could I feel that? *This can't be. They murdered my boss, who was my friend, and they thought they left me for dead.*

Rick wanted to kill them. He was furious!

I wanted to talk to my children. I later learned how they found out about the robbery. Jazz was at home and heard about it on the news. She woke her dad up and called Erika, who was at John's house. She then called DeAnna, who was still at work. John and Erika came to the hospital. Rick had left Jazz at home telling her to call her sister, DeAnna to come get her.

All the news on television said was that one person had been killed, and it showed a video of our shop. Both girls tried to call the shop, but of course no one answered. I couldn't imagine the horror they experienced not knowing if their mother was dead.

Back to the Hospital

The morning sun streaming through the blinds was a welcomed sight. I had not slept, my mind kept replaying everything that had happened.

I climbed out of bed and dressed. Rick drove me back to the hospital. After my X-ray was taken, the doctor came. "Your hand's been shattered. Unfortunately, we can't set it until the swelling goes down," he told me.

Rick drove me to Stu's house to visit the family. All I could say was, "I am sorry."

Stu left behind a loving wife and two beautiful daughters. Stu loved his family and had many friends. What an untimely and senseless death.

I couldn't stay long because of my concussion. My eyes were turning black and blue, and a large bump had emerged on my forehead.

I had a lot of support from DeAnna, Erika, and Jazz. They didn't leave my side for the first couple of days. Ricky was out to sea on an aircraft carrier, his wife Denise kept him updated. Scotty was in prison, I debated whether to tell him what happened to me. He was still part of this family, and needed to know, so I told him. He always called on Sunday. He was so thankful I was ok.

The detectives came by the house with more mug shots. I hadn't been able to recognize the robbers from any of them.

I asked, "Was Stu killed with the first shot?"

"Yes, but the shooter probably didn't think that shot killed him, or they wouldn't have wasted time taping his eyes. We figured the robbers probably thought you were dead since they didn't tape your eyes."

"Why do you think that?"

"The shooter thought he had beaten you to death. That's why he stomped your hand, just to make sure. You said you didn't feel him stomping your hand, I am sure you were unconscious, that probably saved your life.

"No, I never felt it, but I do remember the blows to the back of my head."

"The reason he wanted you dead was because you were the only witness who saw the shooter up close."

That answered my question as to how my hand got shattered.

The following weeks after the robbery-murder, my other boss opened the shop to allow our customers to get their merchandise out of pawn. He asked me to come in for a few hours to help the police with the serial numbers on the guns that were stolen. Under the Bureau of Alcohol, Tobacco, and Firearms (ATF), we had to keep records of who purchased our guns and from whom we purchased them from.

I was very familiar with these records, and I wanted to help as much as possible. Rick stayed with me at the shop, but I could only work about two or three hours at a time.

I recorded all of the serial numbers of the stolen guns, which was estimated to be about fifty. The detectives entered the serial numbers into the national database in order to track them.

One of the detectives said, "With such a large amount of stolen guns, we're sure they'll be sold on the street and will turn up sooner or later."

Several months went by, and not one gun turned up on either the local or on the national level. The detectives wondered if our guns were shipped out of the country.

You're Not Eligible

I had to go weekly back to the hospital for therapy on my hand.

I couldn't receive any workmen's compensation benefits because we were only a small business, and the shop was not required to carry that insurance.

I was told I could get unemployment benefits. What a relief! I went to the unemployment office, and after standing in a very long line, I handed the lady my application for my benefits.

The lady behind the window said, "You're not eligible."

I said, "I've worked for many years, and I've never once made a claim on my unemployment benefits."

"That's not the problem. It's because your hand is in a cast. No one will hire you with a broken hand. You have to be hirable in order to be eligible for unemployment benefits."

I fought back my tears and I wanted to scream. All of my hopes had turned into hopelessness. Now what was I going to do? How would we survive? Fear and despair gripped me.

Sitting in my car, I shouted, "God! God! Why? Why? Where are you? I didn't ask for this. It's not fair. Can just one good thing happen to me?"

My faith had been shattered again. I had children depending on me. Rick was trying, but I knew from past experience that I couldn't depend on him.

I looked at my gas gauge. The needle was almost on empty. I drove back home, still pleading with God to help me. By the time I got home, I knew I was wrong blaming God, so I just thanked him. I reminded myself of the scripture that said in all things give Him praise. I told the Lord I was sorry for being a brat. I knew I had to be obedient to do what the bible said, instead of what I was feeling, which wasn't thankful at all.

Rick stood in the yard talking with his friend Terry, who was a drummer. I didn't want to say anything in front of Terry about my bad news.

I went over where they were standing spoke to Terry. Hugged Rick, I knew he thought everything had turned out okay.

He said, "Terry wants me to do a three-week gig with him starting this weekend."

"Great!" I replied.

Chapter Nineteen

TELEVISION

My faith was tested time and time again. I would love to say I was a champion faith builder, but I had failed many times. Although I failed, He never once failed me.

Again, I learned some very valuable lessons. The Lord stands by His children even when we act like stubborn, rebellious, whiny kids. I wanted to have a pity party, but to be truthful I never could find the time too.

I wanted to have some normalcy in my life, but that never happened either. So as usual, I just kept waking up every morning, saying, "This is the day the Lord has made, and I choose to rejoice in it."

However, I also wondered if I would ever truly rejoice again.

Rick and I were getting along fairly well, and I had accepted that our relationship would always be unstable. I would take the good with the bad.

Every Sunday my mother would call. I'd catch her up on the kids and general things. She missed us and I missed her too.

One Sunday after we ended our conversation, she called right back and asked the same questions, I had already answered. I thought that she had forgotten to tell me something.

"Mom, did you want to tell me something?"

"No." She then ended our conversation.

Two hours later she called again with the same questions. My mother was acting very strange. I sensed something wasn't right.

I asked, "Momma, can I speak to Woodrow?"

"No," she said and hung up.

This was certainly out of character for my mother.

I waited awhile before I called back. Thank God, Woodrow answered. I told him the unusual conversations I'd had with Mom.

He said, "I'm very concerned too. She's not been herself. She's forgetting small things." He chuckled. "Well, we're both in our eighties, so I guess its old age creeping in."

I laughed too. "Keep me updated, especially since you're going in for your prostate operation soon."

"Okay, Marsha."

Construction Begins

One Sunday, Rick decided to go with me to church. On the way home, we passed by a building that was being remodeled.

Rick said, "That's going to be a Christian television station. I'm going to get a job there."

"Right," I said sarcastically. "What makes you think you'll get a job there?"

"I will," he insisted.

I thought, *How ridiculous*.

The weeks went by, and I was still going to the hospital to have therapy on my hand. The doctor had taken the hard cast off and replaced it with a support cast.

I again applied for unemployment, removing the support cast before going into the unemployment office. Thank God, I qualified this time. Within weeks, my first unemployment check arrived.

In order to continue receiving the checks, I was required to look for a job, whether I visited the business in person or called them. I went on several job interviews but never received a call back. I wondered why. I needed to work.

I was thankful for my unemployment check, but it certainly wasn't much. I needed to find a job, although I had not been officially released by my doctor yet.

Memories Lost

One morning, my cousin Robert called me. Robert, what's going on?"

I knew Woodrow had his surgery, and I wondered if something had happened to him.

"Dad is still in the hospital. He's doing fine, but it's your mother I'm worried about. When I dropped her off at the house last night, I went in and secured the house for her. I told her I would be coming by for her in the morning to take her to the hospital.

"This morning I spotted her walking on the sidewalk three blocks from the house. She looked lost. I got her in the car and took her back to the house. Evidently, she had walked out and left the garage door up and the doors unlocked.

"I asked her why she had left the house, and she told me she went out to check the mail. I think you need to come down here. Dad said he would pay for your flight if you can come today. He's worried about leaving her alone."

I told Robert I would fly down as soon as possible. I found a flight that was very cheap, but it was a midnight flight.

I explained the urgency of the situation to Rick, and he agreed that I needed to go. Thank God, I just received my unemployment check the previous day.

I booked my flight and hurriedly packed my suitcase, not knowing the length of my stay. Rick drove me to the airport that night.

When Robert picked me up, he filled me in on some of the things mom had been doing lately. She had been forgetting everyday things, such as how to write a check plus not remembering her phone number. She had a small fender bender just blocks from the house. When the police officer questioned her about running the four-way stop sign, she said she hadn't seen it. This was very disturbing, because she's been driving down that street for years.

When I arrived, Mom was asleep and I didn't wake her.

The next morning, I made sure I was up before Mom. I put on the coffee, and when Mom saw me, she was surprised and confused, but happy I was there.

She asked, "Why did you come without calling me?"

I answered. "Just, an unexpected visit to check on you and Woodrow."

After Woodrow came home from the hospital, he had to be followed up with his treatments, so I was busy with doctor visits. I also made an appointment with Mom's doctor.

The doctor asked her several simple questions which she answered incorrectly or refused to answer. The doctor wanted to talk with Woodrow privately, so I took Mom to the snack bar. She got a coffee, and we sat down and waited for Woodrow.

The doctor confirmed what Woodrow and I thought. Yes, she had the beginning stages of Alzheimer's.

Over several months, I watched my mom become a stranger to me. I didn't get offended when she referred to me as her "good, good friend" instead of her daughter.

I never once tried to get her to join my world. It was easier for me to get in her world. At times, she would say comical things and she would do bizarre things too. Once she packed a suitcase full of cotton balls and Woodrow's underwear to go to Las Vegas. She told me that I was her good, good friend but she could not take me to Las Vegas, I would have to ask my daddy to take me. I agreed that I would ask my dad. I read that most people with Alzheimer's can regress back into their earliest childhood memories.

She often asked me if I knew Uncle Otto who lived in Paris, France. He was a Jewish clockmaker. She asked if I would take her to his house to get a clock.

I answered her *"of course mom"*, I would put her in the car assuring her that I knew where Uncle Otto lived. I would drive her around the block several times, and then we returned to the house. She seemed satisfied.

Of course, I had never heard of Uncle Otto until now. When my mother was a little girl, her parents had told her of an Uncle Otto, a clockmaker and lived in Paris, France. I am sure they shared stories about him.

Years later, to my surprise, I was playing around on line and found an article about Jewish clockmakers in the 1900s. They listed some of their names, and Saville, which was my mother's maiden name, was listed. Most had moved to France.

I thought about Mom, and all the times I had driven her around the block pretending we're going to Paris, to retrieve the clock. I had to smile, after reading this. I wanted to say, *"Mom, you were right about Uncle Otto, the clock and Paris."*

I Got the Job

My trips to Miami became more frequent, and my stays longer as Mom's disease progressed. Rick was supportive and understanding.

While mom and I were washing dishes, which became an hour-long chore. She washed one plate several times. The phone rang I reached over to pick it up with soap suds hands.

"Hello," I said.

"Marsha." I heard Rick's voice. He sounded excited.

"What's going on?"

"I got that job at the Christian television station."

"Really?"

"Yes. I told you I knew I was going to work there," he reminded me.

"Yes, you did." I was happy. "That's great!"

"When do you think you'll be home?"

"I'll be heading home in a few days. How are the girls?"

"Fine."

Of course, I talked with them daily, especially Jazz and whenever I could catch Erika home.

This was good news and the extra money would be such a blessing.

I had quoted Proverbs 16:9 often. About man making his plans, but the Lord directs them. I really felt this was one of those times. I smiled to myself knowing this was an answered prayer. I sensed the Holy Spirit was orchestrating this too.

Eager to return home, I felt my world was about to change again.

When Rick picked me up at the airport, he told me more about his job. He would only work when they needed him.

At times, I would bring him lunch, still wondering why this station had come to Jacksonville, Florida. All I knew was that it was a Christian television station.

He walked me through all the construction going on explaining each detail to me. He took me in the room which was going to be the station's studio. I was amazed at all of the electrical cords hanging from large steel beams that seemed to crisscross each other.

After several weeks, Rick told me the television station would be operational and that they would be airing a live show.

The station manager had asked Rick to help with security the night they were going live on the air. Rick insisted I come with him. As we pulled into the station, the small parking lot was full of cars. The manager met us and gave Rick his instructions. He wanted him to be security for the back lot especially.

A very large semi- truck with a satellite dish on top was parked in the back lot with electrical cords running into the station. I left Rick in charge of the security and walked to the front of the building.

I opened the glass double doors into the lobby than quickly stepped to the right, which placed me in the corner of the lobby. I looked around. This could not be the same building I saw last week. I was amazed that within a week this lobby, which once was a home to electrical cords and sawdust on the floor was now a gorgeous showplace. A beautiful table filled with refreshments and fresh flowers stood in the center of the room.

The lobby was full of people all dressed up, and everything seemed to sparkle with movement. I stood silently in the corner, unnoticed. The room buzzed with excitement. Everyone talked and smiled. I felt as if I was watching a scene from a movie.

The studio doors were shut, but a person dressed in black with headphones would open the doors from the studio and usher someone from the lobby in.

I thought about all those electrical cords that were hanging a week earlier now provided the bright lights for a live television production.

I must have stood by myself for about an hour. I dare not move from the safety of my little corner.

Can You Pray?

Mrs. Mays, the station's secretary, spotted me in the corner. I had talked briefly to her when I brought Rick his lunch. Her husband was the pastor of Southside Assembly, and I had always respected her.

She came directly to me and asked "Marsha, can you pray? I need someone to pray on the prayer phones."

I immediately answered, "No."

She completely ignored my no and gentle pulled me into the adjoining room. "All you need to do is answer the phone by saying, "how may I pray for you?'"

Three older ladies were already on the prayer phones. She told me to sit down at a small cubby hole divided by a two-foot petition that separated each of us. We all had a phone.

A very large glass separated the prayer room from the studio, so we could see directly into it. Mrs. Mays explained to me the different color paper slips that I was to write the on. "The white ones are for salvation, blue for prayer request, pink for praise report, and yellow for anyone wanting information."

Inside the studio, I recognize an evangelist named Benny Hinn. I had heard about him and how the Lord used him for healing.

He was interviewing an older couple. I couldn't hear them, but I knew they were talking about a miraculous healing.

I was still confused. What was Benny Hinn doing here?

My phone rung, I was petrified, but I picked it up. "How may I pray for you?"

"Where is this station located?"

I was relieved, this was easy. "Sir, do you know where Beach Boulevard is?"

"No."

"Do you know where Interstate 95 goes south after the downtown exit?"

"No."

I tried to think of what landmark I could give him. "Do you know where the Hart Bridge is next to the football stadium?"

"No."

Finally, out of desperation, I asked, "Where are you at?"

"Oklahoma."

"Oklahoma!" I almost shouted. I asked again to make sure I heard him right.

"Yes, I am in Oklahoma. Oklahoma City."

"We're in Jacksonville, Florida. You're watching this in Oklahoma?"

"Yes, I am. Praise the Lord," and he hung up.

My first call was thousands of miles from Jacksonville.

I stared at the phone wondering how he knew to call us.

My next caller was a lady with a very thick accent. She asked me to pray for healing. I had prayed only a few times on the phone with one of my friends. Now I had strangers asking me to pray.

Before I prayed, I asked, "Where are you calling from?"

"Puerto Rico," she said.

I said a quick prayer asking the Lord to heal her.

I watched through the glass as the people in the studio waved goodbye. Mrs. Mays came in to let us know that the *Praise the Lord* program had ended. I was relieved. I stayed in the prayer room, didn't want to return to the lobby. It was full of men and women, all smiling and talking. It looked to me as if the lobby had been transformed into shimmering waves of light that bounced from person to person.

I had never experienced this type of an atmosphere. I knew it was God. There was a feeling of love and acceptance that bonded these people together. This was a far cry from the places with which I had known.

Come Back Tomorrow

I was about to leave when Mrs. Mays asked if I could come back tomorrow.

"Tomorrow," I asked, "why?"

"We're having an open house for the public we're inviting them to come visit the station."

"What would I be doing?"

"We'll be giving tours and light refreshments."

I quickly answered, "Yes".

When Rick and I left the station, we were both excited. On the ride home, I told Rick about the phone calls and how surprised I was finding out where they were calling from.

He said, "I talked with the guys in the truck, they told me they were sending the show to satellites in space and it was being sent all over the world."

"Really?" I answered.

He continued to talk but I wasn't listening. My mind kept thinking about what I had just experienced and what tomorrow would bring.

I had a hard time falling asleep. I rehearsed everything that had happened. The one thing that really stood out with me was what I had felt and how the atmosphere felt so different. I couldn't describe what I was feeling except to use the words clean and sparkling.

I was thankful for just being able to participate in small way. I had never been a part of anything pertaining to church.

Finally, I drifted off to sleep.

As I drove to the station the next morning, I thanked God for all the good things He had given me. An outsider looking in may ask, "What good things?"

It wasn't the material things, for which I was grateful for it was the change of heart. I didn't have but one dollar in my purse, but I was happy. How can you explain to someone who has no clue of the precious work that goes on inside of you that only the Holy Spirit can do?

I pushed the glass doors open to the lobby and walked in. The lobby was still set up as it was the previous night, except cookies and lemonade now replaced the nice fruit trays and tasty hors d'oeuvres.

Mrs. Mays greeted me, and we made small talk until Joe, the station manager and chief engineer, walked over to us. He was very likeable and friendly.

He said, "After you help Mrs. Mays, I'll take you around the station, since you'll be doing the tour."

I finished pouring lemonade into the small cups and put more cookies on the trays.

Mrs. Mays said that open house started at ten and will go until four.

"Can you stay the whole time?" she asked.

I said, "I'll stay as long as you need me."

I still did not know any more about this station and was too embarrassed to ask anything either. The marquee outside had the letters WJEB on it, but I did not know what those letters stood for.

After I finished helping Mrs. Mays, Joe asked me to follow him. He took me to the back of the station and showed me the audio booth. I was familiar with this from being in the music studio with Rick. The next room was the director booth, where the director sits and chooses what camera shots would go on the air.

The most impressive room was called Master Control. This ran the whole station and reminded me of the cockpit of an airplane. Small television monitors, strobes, and large racks which held beta tapes that looked like oversized VCR tapes. You could almost feel the electrical current flowing in the air. It was a dream for any electrical geek or technology person, which I definitely was not.

We finally entered the Prayer Room. It brought back memories from the previous night. He didn't have to explain this room to me.

The station's décor was white wicker furniture and colorful cushions that had tropical designs. There were several artificial palm trees, and large colorful vases. Dark green carpet ran throughout the station. Whoever decorated certainly put a Florida theme to it.

I remained in the lobby, waiting for our visitors to arrive. To my surprise, several cars pulled into the parking lot before ten. The first guests were four ladies talking about how great it was for Jacksonville to have a Christian station, especially TBN. I heard them mention the names of Paul and Jan Crouch several times. One asked me if I had ever met them, and I told them no. She went on saying how we were so blessed that Jesus had given us this station. I felt somewhat intimidated, because these ladies knew more about this station than I did.

The open house was in full swing by eleven o'clock with a lot of curious happy people. Mrs. Mays and Joe helped with the many guests we had. I was surprised at how many knew about this station. We decided to break the groups up into seven guests for each of us. The others waited in the lobby, mingling and talking with each other. Their enthusiasm about the station sparked my interest even more. A continuous flow of people came and went throughout the day. I got the same response from everyone which was happy and excited. Still I was puzzled and wondered if I was completely out of the loop.

"This is the heartbeat of this station." I said as I led the groups through the prayer room. I wasn't sure if I explained all the electrical or technology side of the station right, but at least I was sure of prayer room.

Finally, the last group left, and Joe locked the door and I helped Mrs. Mays clean up.

Driving home, I was tired, but I was also re-energized too. I really had enjoyed the day. I felt like I was part of something.

I shared my day with Rick, and he seemed genuinely happy for me. I had a sense of belonging, but I wasn't sure what, where or to whom I belonged to.

Chapter Twenty

FAITHFUL IS MY GOD

Rick was still doing his music and working at the station whenever they needed him, which was not often. One afternoon, I received a phone call from Mrs. Mays.

"Are you interested in being a prayer partner for the live *Praise the Lord* show?"

Without hesitating, I said, "Yes, ma'am."

"Good, you're the first person I've called. Can you come next Saturday?

"Yes, I'll be glad to."

"See you at ten."

I couldn't explain it but each time I thought about the station I got a good feeling. I thought this is strange, but I liked it.

I was still going to therapy for my hand and my concussion was causing me some problems. I had difficulty climbing stairs because I would feel heavy pressure in my head. I knew being a prayer partner brought purpose back in my life, which was good.

Saturday morning came, and I headed to the station. I wondered what was ahead in this adventure. I knew it was going to be good, though.

When I arrived at the station, three ladies and two men were sitting in the lobby. They introduced themselves and asked if I was there for the prayer partners training.

Mrs. Mays entered the lobby with an attractive black lady. She introduced her as Colette and that she was going to train us.

Colette led the six of us into the prayer room. She told us that we would be answering the phones during the live *Praise the Lord* show.

I had an advantage over the others, since I had already done this. The training didn't take long, and soon I was on my way home. This was going to be a new experience for me. Colette said that we were called Prayer Partners and we volunteered our time on Tuesday and Friday from eleven to one-thirty.

When Tuesday morning came, I was overjoyed and filled with a sense of pride. When I arrived, pastors and guests were already in the lobby.

Colette was busy getting ready for the show. The other prayer partners were waiting in the prayer room. We all were excited and full of anticipation. We had fifteen minutes before the live show, so we all joined hands and prayed.

When the show started, we sat in our chairs with big smiles. The phones began to ring. All lines were full. We were all praying and writing their requests.

When the show ended, we placed the prayer requests in the prayer basket, held them up to the Lord, and prayed again. My work for the Lord had begun, and I was overjoyed.

I had been praying for months and felt I was gaining self-confidence that the Lord had me where I was supposed to be. One morning as I listened to a woman pour out her heart concerning a situation she was facing, I heard inside of me "Tell her I heard her this morning as she poured her coffee in her red coffee mug."

I thought I must be losing it. I can't tell this woman this. What was happening? I couldn't concentrate on what she asked me to pray about because this impression continued to get stronger as if someone had taken over me and wouldn't stop talking to me. I thought maybe this was God.

Finally, I said, "I have to tell you something. The Lord wants you to know …" and I repeated what I had heard verbatim.

She didn't say anything for a few seconds. I thought I had screwed up. This caller needed prayer, and I just blurted out some ridiculous statement.

She started crying, not out of sorrow, but she began to praise God. She said, "Every morning I drink my coffee out of a red coffee mug."

I was more surprised than she was, and believe me, I rejoiced with her. God had spoken through me. Never had I experienced anything like that.

The Lord begin to use me several different times to speak to callers who really needed confirmation that He loved them and knew them personally.

One that really stood out was a lady who called several times. Each time, it was I who received the call. She was afraid of her husband. I knew from previous phone calls they had children. He was not working, and it was a very volatile situation.

We prayed together and bound up the devil. I always applied the blood of Jesus over her and her household. I knew in my spirit, this lady really needed protection.

After the show ended, we always took the phone receiver off the hook and unplugged the phones before we left. I was about to walk out when the phone rang without being plugged in.

I thought, *how can this be?*

I plugged it back in and picked it up, thinking there must be a mix up. To my surprise, this lady was on the other end. She was desperate. She had rushed home, hoping to reach our prayer line. Of course, she recognized my voice. She told me that her husband had planned to kill them. He told her something had stopped him, and he couldn't go through with his plan.

We rejoiced, but she was still not out of danger. The Spirit of God began to speak through me to her. "Your husband will be in ministry, and he will be on the *Praise the Lord* show sharing this testimony."

I was completely shocked at what came out of my mouth. Her husband did not believe in God, and in ministry seemed ridiculous. We had been praying for his salvation for several months.

We both cried and rejoiced. I thought, *either this is God, or I'm just a false prophet, but I have never and still will not say I am a prophet by any means.* I say, that I am just God's mailman. I deliver the envelope, and the Lord writes the letter. I take no credit, nor am I responsible for anything.

I had just experienced a supernatural work of the Holy Spirit. Why? Because He loved this lady so much that He allowed me to linger long enough to answer a phone that had no connection and speak to one woman who needed a word from God. Oh! That wonderful love of the Father that transcends everything to speak to just one of His children.

A year later, guess what? Yep, that lady and her husband sat on the *Praise the Lord* show giving their testimony. Everything the Lord spoke had come to pass. They were in ministry together. This taught me that nothing is impossible for God, even in the darkest place, and never give up regardless of what you see or hear.

Permanent Position

Colette had a degree in broadcasting and was instrumental in creating the live *Praise the Lord* show and our other in-house production. Before taking maternity leave with her first child, she was training one of our prayer partners to take her place while she was out.

The lady she was training had a college degree and would do a good job. One of our older prayer ladies named Christine said, "Marsha, this is supposed to be your job."

I had the utmost respect for Christine. She stood four-foot seven and was ninety years young. She had been widowed at an early age. She visited a missionary friend of hers in Honduras and ended up living there and built nine churches.

We became good friends. She mentored me in so many ways.

I told her, "Christine, I respect you, but this time you're not hearing from God."

Several weeks went by, and I knew the lady being trained was having a difficult time with her new position. She asked me to pray for her, she told me she didn't feel this was her job. I tried to reassure her, especially if this is what God wanted for her.

Christine's words kept coming into my spirit, and I rebuked them, thinking 'this is my flesh or the devil.' But those words would not leave me.

On a Tuesday, as I was heading to the station, I told the Lord, "Either this is you telling me that I am to take this position, or it is the devil. I need to know."

Colette asked if I could stay after the show because she and Joe, the manager, wanted to talk to me.

Sure enough, they both asked me if I would take over for Colette. Without hesitation I said, "Of course."

Driving home, I was beyond myself. All I could do was smile. I knew this was from God.

When I got home, I had received my last unemployment check. I was praising and worshipping the Lord right there in my living room, just me and God. I'm not sure if I can articulate what I experienced, I actually felt the love of God, His beautiful Presence. His love was so strong that my physical body couldn't handle it. It was only for a split second but it was amazing.

The Bible says our bodies will be changed, and now I understood why. His love is so powerful, you can't contain it. The experience was too much. I had so many different emotions. I couldn't even describe them. This was a different dimension than I had ever experienced. His love was overwhelming. How could Jesus be so good to me? From all my failures, fears, doubts, and anger, I was a big mess, but yet He allowed me to feel His unconditional love.

About an hour after experiencing this, I somehow returned to normal when the phone rang. Before I picked it up, I knew who and why the person on the other end was calling.

I answered, "Hello?"

Sure enough, it was Colette. Before she could say anything, I said, "Colette, don't say what I think you're going to say."

She said, "I went to my doctor's appointment today, and he is putting me in the hospital and inducing labor on Sunday. I am sorry, but I will not be able to train you. In the bottom file cabinet, you'll find everything you'll need for the *Praise the Lord* Show. Look in my Day Timer book, where I've written the Pastors and guests' names and phone numbers for our Christmas show. You will need to call and confirm their dates for the live Christmas show."

Thank God, I had just experienced what I did because this was way out of my league. I had never thought of doing anything in television, especially a two-hour live show twice a week. This had never entered my mind.

After hanging up from Colette, I asked, "God, are you sure I can do this?"

I didn't know what God was up to. At this point in my life, I knew He was full of surprises, but was I ready.

I knew He had just begun His marvelous work in me and through me. I was nothing exceptional, but He was. I felt that He and I were about to embark on a series of adventures that would take me into a deeper relationship and that He was about to teach me how to be led by His Spirit.

I knew the Holy Spirit was speaking to me. I knew He was going to test me to trust Him more than before. The bible said "We go from glory to glory." But what would be asked of me? What if I failed Him? What if I did not want to do what He asked? All these thoughts and many more ran through my mind.

Could He trust me that was a big issue for me? Could I be trusted? I had heard well-meaning Christians say "I wish God would speak to me, I would do anything He wanted me too." I knew they were well meaning but I also knew that they were not serious, either. I would say "I hope God doesn't speak to me." "What! Marsha!" they would respond. "Because when God speaks to me I have to do what He asks."

The Lord was already speaking to me but I told no one. Trinity Broadcasting Network was just the beginning of another *Destiny Driven by Love* not for me but for others. I shivered inside with expectancy of the unknown but I was willing to lay my life down for Him. The question was would I have too? That I didn't know.

About the Author

MARSHA GEOGHAGAN

Marsha Geoghagan is an author who has lived a life many thought only existed in movies. Her experiences created her character and allowed God to mold her into the person she is today, yet she admits that He is still working on her and will be until the day she meets Him face to face.

Marsha has been employed by WJEB-TV 59, an affiliate station of Trinity Broadcasting Network since 1992. While there, she has taken on the role of, producer, secretary, and receptionist, and has manned the prayer line. She contributes her years with this television network as her introduction into ministry.

She has since expanded her ministry service. She has traveled and ministered in Israel, Cuba, Swaziland, and throughout the United States. Additionally, Marsha is currently the vice president of the Northeast Florida Aglow International and is its vice president of Leadership Development. She also founded and hosted the television talk show *For Such a Time as This* on Comcast 99.

Her anointing brings in a prophetic voice. Her desire it to have permanent life changes in the spirit realm and to establish and equip all to walk in their end-time anointing.

Marsha and her husband Lee attend Orange Park Celebration Church where Lee serves as an usher, and she serves on the prayer team and the church's Care Partner Ministry. She has five grown children, nine grandchildren, and three great-grandchildren.

www.ingramcontent.com/pod-product-compliance
Lightning Source LLC
Chambersburg PA
CBHW021144080526
44588CB00008B/204